Power Tools for Business Writing

Julie G. Levitt

*Business Consultant, Trainer,
and National Presenter
Former Supervisor with
Boise State University, Boise, Idaho*

Jeff Craig

*Corporate Training Developer
and Business Consultant,
International Fortune 500 Company*

SOUTH-WESTERN
CENGAGE Learning

Australia • Brazil • Japan • Korea • Mexico • Singapore • Spain • United Kingdom • United States

SOUTH-WESTERN
CENGAGE Learning

Power Tools for Business Writing
Julie Levitt and Jeff Craig

VP/Editorial Director: Jack W. Calhoun

VP/Editor-in-Chief: Karen Schmohe

Acquisitions Editor: Jane Phelan

Consulting Editor: Marianne Miller

Production Editor: Cami Cacciatore

Production Service: Cadmus
Professional Communications

Art Director: Stacy Jenkins Shirley

Internal and Cover Designer:
Beckmeyer Design, Inc.

Cover Images: Getty Images;
iStockphoto

Photo Researcher: Darren Wright

Senior First Print Buyer: Doug Wilke

For product information and technology assistance, contact us at **Cengage Learning Customer & Sales Support, 1-800-354-9706**

For permission to use material from this text or product, submit all requests online at **www.cengage.com/permissions** Further permissions questions can be emailed to **permissionrequest@cengage.com**

U.S. Student Edition:
ISBN-13: 978-0-538-72875-1
ISBN-10: 0-538-72875-2

South-Western Cengage Learning
5191 Natorp Boulevard
Mason, OH 45040
USA

Cengage Learning is a leading provider of customized learning solutions with office locations around the globe, including Singapore, the United Kingdom, Australia, Mexico, Brazil, and Japan. Locate your local office at: **international.cengage.com/region**.

Cengage Learning products are represented in Canada by Nelson Education Ltd.

For your course and learning solutions, visit **www.cengage.com**.

Purchase any of our products at your local college store or at our preferred online store **www.ichapters.com**.

Printed in the United States of America
3 4 5 6 7   12 11 10 09

CONTENTS

APPENDIX

PREFACE

IF YOU ONLY HAVE 12 HOURS TO IMPROVE YOUR WRITING SUBSTANTIALLY, THIS IS THE BOOK FOR YOU!

Welcome to *Power Tools for Business Writing*, the results-oriented program that boosts writing skills by 35 percent in just 12 to 15 hours. Improvement is immediate, substantial, and measurable.

Powerful Results

The goal of helping users develop practical career-building skills emphasized in Julie Griffin Levitt's *Your Career: How to Make it Happen* is also the primary goal of this book. This Power Tools formula for writing success works—a phenomenal **35 percent average improvement** in writing skills is validated through comparison of pretest and posttest scores over ten years.

You can also achieve this level of improvement or better. You will learn to write quickly and confidently and with positive impact. The Power Tools approach is proven to produce exceptional results.

> *Power Tools for Business Writing* improves writing quickly and dramatically.
>
> A phenomenal **35 percent average improvement** in writing skills is validated through comparison of pretest and posttest scores over ten years.

Powerful Outcomes

- Jump-start your message, overcome writer's block, and write faster.
- Organize your message for impact.
- Plug into clear, concise, and correct writing.
- Format business documents correctly.
- Communicate with confidence.
- Quickly master the correct use of commas, colons, and semicolons.
- Proofread and edit to produce quality documents.

Powerful Benefits

- **Rapid, substantial improvement of writing skills.** The program focuses on the practical writing skills and techniques that most quickly and substantially strengthen business documents. Through more than ten years of use in educational and business training courses, the content has been tested and perfected to produce exceptional improvement in writing skills.

- **Clear, understandable, and usable content.** This book features easy, clear content that is quickly understood and retained and immediately usable to improve writing skill.

Like the thousands who have successfully used the Power Tools formula over the last decade, soon you will be saying:

- "This is the best writing course I have taken. I now know how to overcome writer's block, organize content, and develop a forceful message."

- "The frequent review of key concepts helps me to remember and apply them in my writing."

- "I have never taken such a practical writing course."

- "This course is fun! This subject has never been so clearly explained—it's easy to understand and to apply immediately."

- **Dynamic slides featuring concept development exercises.** The professionally developed slides incorporate sound pedagogy with emphasis on clear concept presentation, review, and application exercises to reinforce learning. They energize participants and focus their attention.

- **Developed by writing and educational experts.** The extensive university instruction and corporate training expertise of both authors, Julie Griffin Levitt and Jeff Craig, result in superior instructional content, teaching strategies, learning activities, and program materials.

FOCUS CENTERED ON RESULTS-ORIENTED WRITING SKILLS

In today's global business environment, clear, concise communications translate into increased profits. Many people work in virtual teams separated by time zones, cultures, and language, all of which pose challenges to clear and timely communication. This program reflects several years of successfully teaching people to communicate clearly and efficiently, thereby increasing productivity.

PRACTICAL APPROACH IMPROVES WRITING QUICKLY

The following are typical areas of concern for people who want to improve their business writing skills:

- Where do I put the comma?

- How do I express my ideas concisely?

- How do I organize my ideas quickly?

- How can I write persuasively?

Those topics are addressed in the program along with the practical topics found to result in the greatest improvement in business writing during a short-term course.

The concepts are presented in a reader-friendly style, and writing activities are incorporated throughout the course to reinforce the concepts.

Focus Builds Skill Quickly

Power Tools for Business Writing first presents the proven formula for getting the message started quickly and efficiently:

- Overcoming writer's block (offers easy techniques that work)
- Organizing the message for optimum impact (capitalizes on natural thinking patterns)

The focus then shifts to a quick review of basic grammar and writing foundations. The content is direct and easy to understand. The style is informal and energizing.

- Grammar foundations
- Punctuation
- Sentence and paragraph structure

The focus then turns to results-oriented writing strategies:

- Writing quickly and efficiently
- Writing persuasively
- Writing concisely
- Formatting business documents correctly
- Proofreading and editing

Program Components Reinforce Learning

The success of this results-oriented writing program centers on the following key components:

Text-Workbook

The text-workbook serves three functions for participants: (1) to be used when completing course activities, (2) to serve as a study guide, and (3) to be used as a desk reference for future writing needs. Participants report that the content is easy to grasp and apply to real-world business situations. The features of this component are as follows:

- Learning objectives are presented at the beginning of each chapter.
- Concepts are presented in guided learning style.
- Activities reinforce learning. Students apply the concepts in application exercises to reinforce learning.
- Concept Reviews periodically reinforce important concepts.
- Tips periodically emphasize important ideas

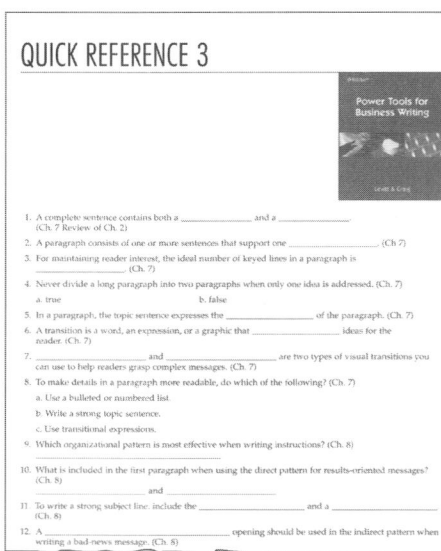

Convenient Quick References

Four convenient forms summarize the core concepts of the entire program. Participants fill in these "crib sheets" for each class session. These forms:

- Provide a quick reference throughout the course and in the future to the key concepts and skills that improve writing quickly.

- May be posted at the participants' work or home writing areas as reminders to apply the new techniques as they write documents between sessions.

- May be used as a study guide for the quizzes and the final posttest.

Quality Instructor Materials

The comprehensive instructor materials are designed for easy adaptation to a variety of programs. An Instructor's Resource CD (IRCD) contains the following program components:

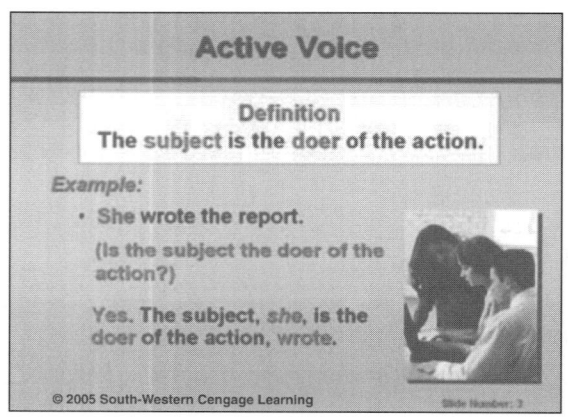

- **Retention-boosting slides.** The distinctive PowerPoint® slides clearly introduce, reinforce, and test the program concepts. Answers to all activities are provided in the slides. Eye-appealing graphics and animation along with sound clips are incorporated to project professionalism, attract and sustain participant attention, and increase retention through quality visual reinforcement. Selected slides also include animated characters to energize the instruction.

- **Instructor Notes for PowerPoint slides.** Selected slides contain Instructor Notes with value-added coaching questions as well as supplemental teaching content to make the instructor's job easier.

- **Comprehensive Instructor's Manual, Session Preparation Guides, and Lesson Plans.** The Instructor's Manual explains the program components and the recommended teaching methods and activities. The Session Preparation Guides provide complete guidelines for preparing to teach each session.

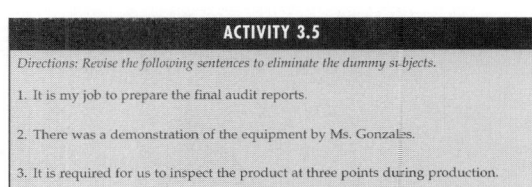

Session 3 Lesson Plan

Session 3 Lesson Plan (3 hours) (See Session 3 Preparation Guide for details)	Clock Time (You Fill In)	Time Estimates	Slide #
1. **Complete all Preparation Checklist Items** (Load slides, distribute handouts, etc.)		(preclass activities)	
2. **Review Answers to Quick Reference 1 (QR1)** Use hard copy answer key or QR1 key on slides to review and reinforce QR1concepts.		(2.) 15 min.	QR1 Review and Answer Key slides
3. **Review Answers to Quick Reference 2 (QR2)** Use hard copy answer key or QR2 key on slides to review QR2 and prepare for Quiz 2.		(3.) 15 min.	QR2 Review and Answer Key slides
4. **Administer Quiz 2** Distribute. Tell participants to answer questions quickly. Correct in class or collect and correct yourself.		(4.) 15 min. 45 min. Total Time Elapsed	

Quality Evaluation! *Power Tools for Business Writing* provides immediate, measurable improvement!

ACTIVITY 3.5

Directions: Revise the following sentences to eliminate the dummy subjects.

1. It is my job to prepare the final audit reports.

2. There was a demonstration of the equipment by Ms. Gonzales.

3. It is required for us to inspect the product at three points during production.

- **Lesson Plans for each class session.** Individual lesson plans are provided for each teaching session. The plans are designed as a brief session overview for in-class reference. These plans contain lists of topics for each session along with time frames for delivery of each topic and references to related slide and text-workbook page numbers. The Lesson Plans are found on the IRCD in the Lesson Plans folder.

- **Participant evaluation package.** The Pretest and Posttest measure participants' achievement of the course learning objectives. Session review quizzes provide periodic measurement of learning and reinforce retention of the key program concepts.

Guided and Independent Writing Practice Activities

Writing application practice is provided for all key concepts. During guided practice, the instructor monitors participants as they practice key writing skills to ensure that they use the skill correctly. Independent practice is just that, independent. Participants practice skills between classes.

Content Organized for Ease of Use

The *Power Tools for Business Writing* program is organized to move from basic grammar and language foundations to document writing and formatting techniques. However, each chapter can stand independently from the other chapters, making the program flexible to meet individual course or workshop needs.

CHAPTER 1

Quick Starting Tools

Objectives

After completing Chapter 1, you will be able to:

- Knock out writer's block.
- Cluster ideas to generate ideas quickly.
- Maintain writing momentum.
- Write an efficient first draft.

WRITER'S BLOCK

The keys to achieving good writing momentum are getting ready to write, focusing first on the right-brain activity (generating ideas), and avoiding interruptions. This section explains how to achieve those goals efficiently.

Have you ever experienced writer's block? Did you find the block frustrating and unproductive because it wasted precious time? Follow these guidelines to avoid writer's block and to start your writing projects with ease:

1. **Assemble references and materials.** Clear space and gather relevant references, such as previous correspondence and research materials. Assemble other writing materials you may need.

2. **Set aside time, and avoid interruptions.** Set aside a predefined block of time for writing, and advise those you work with that you are not to be interrupted. If you write frequently, set aside a routine block of time. Resist distractions—discipline is a powerful ally to good writers.

3. **Set a deadline.** If you don't have a deadline, set one up front. If you're working on a big project, make a commitment to someone and write it on your calendar. Deadlines are great motivators.

4. **Write at your peak time.** Are you a morning, afternoon, or evening person? Plan to write when you're functioning at optimum level.

5. **Talk your thoughts out first.** Say your message aloud to someone willing to act as a sounding board. This is a terrific strategy for getting your thoughts to jell.

6. **Treat yourself.** If everything else fails, have a cookie or whatever treat soothes your "Savage Writer's Block Beast."

 TIP *When taking a break, stop writing in the middle of a sentence or paragraph that has clear direction. When you resume your writing, you'll be in the middle of a thought, ready to go, instead of trying to think of what to write next. This gives you an automatic restarting point that sustains your writing momentum.*

CLUSTERING TO GENERATE IDEAS

You can create and sustain your writing momentum by using the clustering technique to capture initial ideas for a written message. Clustering is a free-association thought process that focuses on the right brain. A primary function of the right brain is to generate creative ideas. Consequently, clustering works naturally with the right brain to get ideas flowing quickly. It capitalizes on the ability of the right brain to develop thought patterns and associations, without stopping to analyze. The purpose of clustering is to generate initial ideas and rough draft content efficiently, not to analyze or edit your thoughts.

Conversely, outlining, the traditional method of creating ideas, is both a left- and right-brain activity. The function of the left brain is to analyze. In traditional outlining, the right brain generates an idea and the left brain interrupts to analyze and decide where the idea should be placed in the outline. As a starting point, traditional outlining is not efficient. This process risks loss of ideas because it interrupts the idea-generating process to determine the order of the content. Most people can't effectively use both sides of the brain simultaneously.

When writing, focus the functions of your left and right brain to your advantage. First, use only the right brain in clustering your ideas to generate a rough outline of the content for your message. Then use your left brain to organize and edit your rough outline.

Sometimes the ideas you generate from clustering will be adequate to develop your final written message. With long or complex messages, you may need a second step: developing a formal outline from your original cluster.

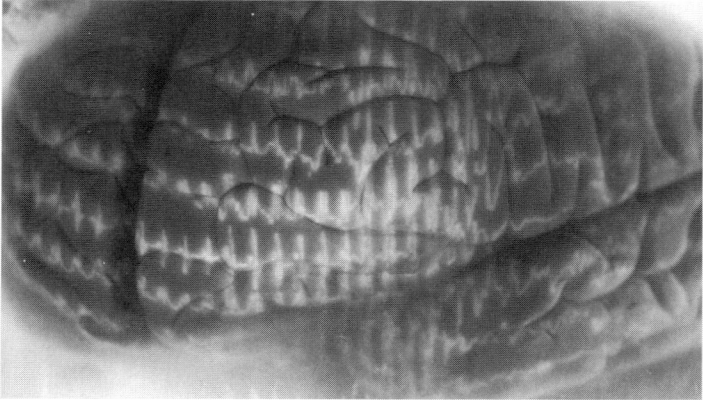

Follow Steps to Cluster Ideas

Use the following steps to stimulate your normal creative thought processes and to get your writing swiftly under way. Remember that clustering is designed to generate initial ideas and draft content, not to analyze or edit your thoughts.

1. Begin with a blank piece of paper, a pen or pencil, and the main topic of your message.

2. Jot down the main topic (a word or phrase) in the middle of your paper, and draw a circle around it.

3. Use your right brain to contemplate and develop this topic freely.

4. In a circle around your main topic, jot down every key idea that emerges and circle each of these thoughts.

5. Don't organize or correct these key ideas, and don't write complete sentences; just get them down in writing.

6. Use your left brain to review the key ideas that have emerged from your clustering. Add items that need to be included, and delete any that are irrelevant.

7. Create a rough outline by numbering your clustered ideas in the most logical order for developing your message. This rough outline may be an adequate guide for composing your communication. It can also be used as a guide for developing a traditional outline.

8. Write a *focus statement* (one that sums up the purpose of the message). The focus statement should express your purpose in one sentence. If you can't express the purpose in one sentence, it is likely not clear enough for a typical business document. This statement often becomes the first sentence or the essence or focus of the first paragraph.

   Quickly draft your focus statement (working from the right brain); then review and refine or polish the statement carefully using the left brain. Strive to convey a brief, clear picture of your primary message. A strong focus statement improves the reader's ability to comprehend your message quickly, and this statement focuses your entire message.

Clustering Alternative 1. Consider clustering your ideas using a word processor. The trick, however, is to write your ideas with the screen turned off. This technique prohibits your logical left brain from interrupting your free-flowing thoughts to analyze them.

Clustering Alternative 2. Dictating is another effective clustering approach. Dictate your ideas as you generate them, listen to them, and then transfer key ideas to paper or a word processor.

ACTIVITY 1.1

Directions: You have just won the Mega Lottery, and you have enough money to do anything you want for the rest of your life. Cluster ideas for an article explaining what you will do with the money. Follow these steps to complete this activity:

1. Contemplate what you will do with the lottery money. At the bottom of the page, create a cluster of your ideas (right-brain activity).

2. Review the cluster, add topics that are missing, and delete any unnecessary topics (left-brain activity).

3. Number the topics in order of the best development for your message (left-brain activity).

4. Write a focus statement for your article that sums up the essence of the message (right-brain activity).

TECHNIQUES FOR MAINTAINING MOMENTUM

Maintaining writing momentum means keeping your ideas flowing without interruption. When drafting your message, focus on using your creative right brain to generate ideas. Also use the following technique to avoid losing your train of thought when you can't think of the right word or phrase:

- Key the first word(s) that come to mind.
- Key a blank line after the word(s) as a reminder to follow up.
- Keep writing to maintain your momentum and stimulate thoughts that are jelling.

This technique keeps your ideas flowing, using your creative right brain to generate the draft without losing thoughts and momentum.

Example: Our engineers *evaluate* the performance _____ data.

Revision: Our engineers *analyze* the performance data.

EFFICIENT FIRST DRAFT

You'll gain significant benefits from developing a spontaneous rough draft. The *spontaneous writing process* is also referred to as *automatic writing* or *freewriting*. The goal is to elaborate freely on your key ideas—to unload your thoughts on paper without hesitation. As in clustering, spontaneous rough drafting is efficient because it capitalizes on the creativity of the right brain. Spontaneous drafting speeds the process of developing key ideas, enhances the creative content and personal quality of writing, and makes the entire writing process easier.

Start with Clustered Outline and Focus Statement

Review the ideas that emerge from your clustering activity. Add any items that help make your message complete, and eliminate items that are irrelevant. Then renumber your ideas as necessary to achieve the most logical order for developing a spontaneous draft of your message.

Use Guidelines to Create Rough Draft

Writing spontaneously, work from your right brain to generate as many thoughts as possible for each point of your rough outline. When you complete your rough draft, you'll have a solid framework of original ideas for writing a forceful message.

Follow these guidelines to create a strong working draft:

1. Refer to the cluster of ideas you organized, and write a spontaneous rough draft of your message. The draft doesn't have to be correct—*aim for content*, not perfection.

2. Begin by expanding on each of your key ideas, and write quickly without pausing to analyze.

3. Write in phrases, not complete sentences. This allows you to grasp ideas rapidly and keep your thoughts rolling.

4. Avoid analyzing the content. Don't make changes in wording. Don't correct grammar or spelling.

5. Spend about five minutes generating the spontaneous draft of an average-length letter.

6. Use this draft as a starting point for polishing your final message.

ACTIVITY 1.2

Directions: Turn to page 103; and review the directions for completing the Power Tools Writing Project, the main writing assignment for this course. Then get started on the assignment in class by doing the following:

1. Cluster ideas for a document you need or want to write.

2. Review the cluster, add topics that are missing, and delete any unnecessary topics.

3. Number the topics in order of the best development for your message.

4. Write a focus statement for your document that sums up the essence of the message.

5. Rough-draft three paragraphs of your document in class.

PROOF POINT!

Directions: Follow the steps listed below to complete this clustering exercise.

1. Review the clustering guidelines provided earlier in this chapter.

2. Review the following cluster of ideas to be incorporated in a proposal. The proposal is to explain training workshops to be offered on the subject of public speaking. Assume you are a trainer who has discussed public-speaking training needs with Axion Company. That company now wants you to submit a written proposal outlining the training program you will provide.

3. Number the clustered items in the most logical order of development for the proposal.

4. Write a focus statement you could use in the first paragraph to express the main idea or purpose of the message.

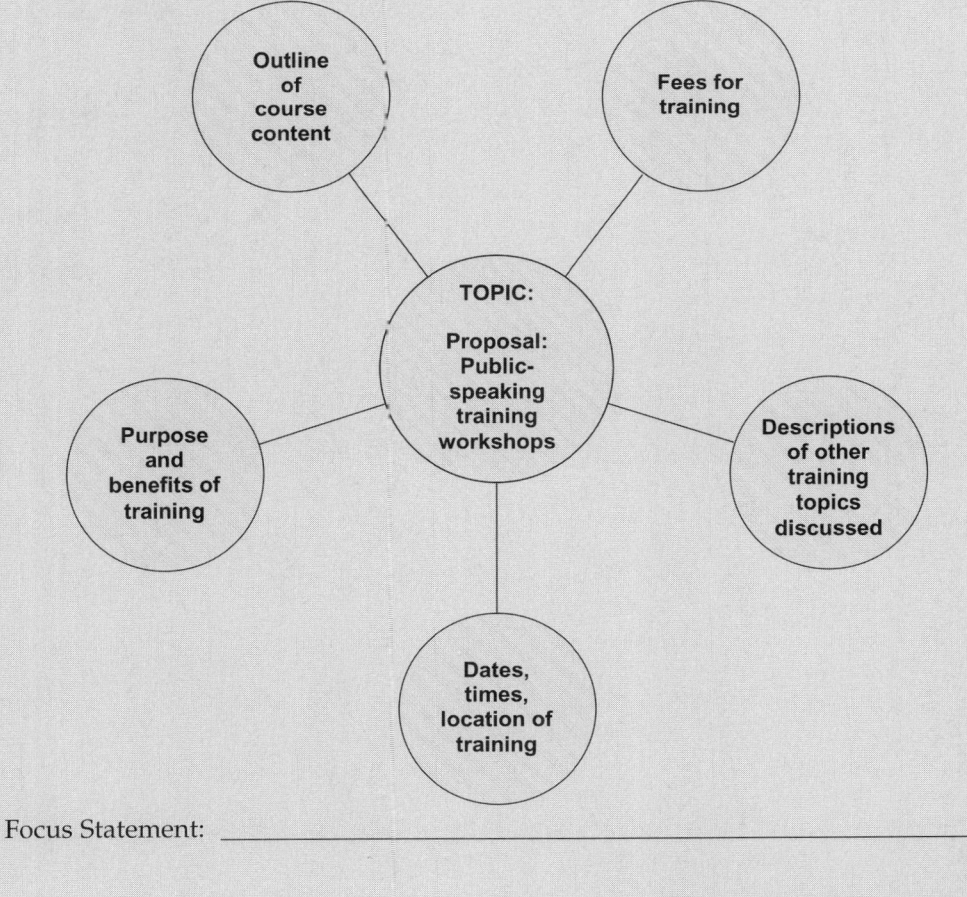

Focus Statement: _____

_____

Grammar Foundations

Objectives

After completing Chapter 2, you will be able to:

- Identify important grammar elements.
- Compose complete sentences.
- Correct common subject and verb agreement errors.

IMPORTANT GRAMMAR ELEMENTS

You can improve the clarity and correctness of your writing by using the key parts cf speech and important sentence elements correctly.

Subject

The **subject** is one of the following:

1. The main doer of the action

2. The main thing or person described

In the first example below, the subject is underlined once. What are the subjects in the next two examples?

- <u>Mark</u> writes reports.

- The report is short.

- Silvia will bring the report tomorrow.

ACTIVITY 2.1

Directions: Underline the subject in each of the following sentences.

1. Our manager will present his proposal at the meeting.

2. The marketing staff and my assistant will review your proposal today.

CLAD
Command
Location
Action
Description

Verb

A **verb:**

1. Describes what the subject does.

2. Links to words that describe the subject.

The acronym shown at the left makes it easy to remember the functions of a verb.

In the following examples, the verb is underlined twice.

- <u>Prepare</u> a shipment list for each product. (commands—the subject *you* is understood)

- We <u>are</u> in the conference room. (indicates location)

- Lee <u>writes</u> technical proposals. (indicates action)

- Mario <u>is</u> a sales representative. (describes)

 NOTE   *A helping verb may be used with a main verb as in the example below:*

We <u>are preparing</u> the report. (*Preparing* is the main verb, indicating action. It is preceded by a form of the helping verb *be*. Some forms of the verb *be* include *is, are, was, were,* and *will be*. *Are* is the helping verb in this sentence.)

ACTIVITY 2.2

Directions: Circle the subject and underline the verb twice in each of the following sentences.

1. The floor supervisors train all new hires.

2. Send a copy of the report to all board members today.

Ing as a Gerund

A **gerund** is a word that ends in *ing* and is used only as a noun. A gerund functions in the sentence as a subject or an object.

- <u>Bicycling</u> is good exercise.
  (subject)

- He enjoys <u>teaching</u>.
       (object)

Ing as a Verb Form

A word ending in *ing* is a verb if it is directly preceded by some form of the helping verb *be*. Some forms of the helping verb *be* include *is, are, am, were, has been,* and *will be*.

- <u>We</u> <u>are selling</u> commercial office space in the downtown area.
  (*We* = the doer; *are* = the helping verb; *are selling* = the complete verb)

- <u>Sue</u> <u>was skiing</u> in Wyoming.

ACTIVITY 2.3

Directions: Classify each ing *word in the following sentences as a verb or a gerund. If the word is a verb, write* V *on the line. If it is a gerund, write* G.

1. ____ The director prefers *meeting* in the main conference room.

2. ____ *Programming* computers is his hobby.

3. ____ She is *programming* my computer today.

4. ____ *Testing* the electronic circuit is a complex task.

Infinitive

An **infinitive** consists of *to* plus a verb. An infinitive is a distinctly separate part of speech; it is *not* a verb.

- He plans *to attend* the conference in London.

- *To reduce* grammatical errors, always use grammar-checking software.

ACTIVITY 2.4

Directions: Circle the verbs in the following sentences.

1. The committee plans to develop a prototype model within two weeks.

2. Carefully monitoring the production process to verify quality control checks.

Clause

A **clause** is a group of words that contains a subject and a verb. **Independent clauses** express a complete thought and can stand alone as a complete sentence.

- Josh gave a good presentation because he prepared well.
  (*Josh gave a good presentation* = independent clause)

Dependent clauses do not express a complete thought even though they contain a subject and a verb. Dependent clauses require other elements in order to be complete or to make sense.

Dependent clauses are introduced by **subordinating conjunctions,** "flag words," including *if, after, because, before, when, until, since,* and *although;* by the relative pronouns *who, whom, that,* and *which;* or by the conjunctions *how, why, that,* and *what.*

- *Before we left for the meeting,* we reviewed the objectives carefully.
     (dependent clause)   (independent clause)

- If you study diligently, you should pass the exam.

- I will prepare a summary of recommendations after I complete the research.

 TIP *When a dependent clause comes first, a comma immediately follows it. When the dependent clause comes last, no comma is used.*

ACTIVITY 2.5

Directions: On the first line, write an independent clause. On the second line, write a dependent clause.

_____

_____

Coordinating Conjunction, "Little Word"

Coordinating conjunctions join independent clauses of a compound sentence. The primary coordinating conjunctions are *yet, or, but,* and *and*.

The acronym shown at the left makes it easy to remember the primary coordinating conjunctions, or "little words":

- Erisa is in law school, **and** Ken is studying medicine.
  The word *and* (coordinating conjunction) joins independent but related clauses of a compound sentence.

- I would like to go with you to the conference, **but** I have a conflicting commitment.

YOBA
Yet
Or
But
And

ACTIVITY 2.6

Directions: Insert a "little word" to join the two independent clauses below. Then on the blank line, compose your own sentence using a "little word" to join two independent clauses.

I have just won one million dollars. I am excited about spending it.

_____

Phrase

A **phrase** is a group of words that does not contain both a subject and a verb. A phrase may contain one or the other, but it does not contain both.

- *As agreed last week,* the interview team will select the final candidate.

- *In the field of office automation,* competition is increasing.

COMPLETE SENTENCES

Writing correct sentences is essential to projecting a professional business image. This section explains how to identify the required elements of correct sentence structure.

Sentence

A **sentence** is a word or group of words that:

1. Expresses a complete thought.

2. Contains both a *subject* and a *verb*. (The subject *you* may be understood in a command, as in the following example of the shortest possible complete sentence: *Go.*)

3. Contains at least one *independent clause.*

ACTIVITY 2.7

Directions: Write C on the line to indicate a complete sentence. Write I to indicate an incomplete sentence.

1. Working together as a team. _____

2. Working together as a team is exciting. _____

3. We are working together as a team. _____

4. Work together as a team. _____

SUBJECT

The subject is the doer of the action or the main person, thing, concept, or quality described. Each sentence and each independent clause must have both a subject and a verb.

VERB

The verb indicates command, action, location, or description.

- Julio writes the summary reports for our team.

- She is writing the marketing plan.
  This sentence contains the helping verb *is* plus the main verb *writing*. Examples of other helping verbs include *has/have* (She has written the marketing plan) and *will/would* (She will write the marketing plan).

- Bind the annual report on the left side.

- He is in Boston attending a training program.

Simple Sentence

A **simple sentence** contains one independent clause. (Remember that an independent clause contains a subject and a verb and expresses a complete thought.) The subject may be singular or compound.

- Mary prepared the budget.
  (singular subject, *Mary*)

- Mary and Takeo prepared the budget together.
  (compound subject, *Mary and Takeo*)

Compound Sentence

A **compound sentence** contains two or more independent clauses. A compound sentence has more than one subject because it has more than one clause.

- <u>Devon</u> spoke on the topic of quality assurance, and the <u>audience</u> was responsive.

Complex Sentence

A **complex sentence** contains one independent clause and one dependent clause.

In the following examples, the subordinating conjunctions ("flag words") are shown in italics. Also notice that a comma is used at the end of the dependent clause when the dependent clause comes first in a complex sentence.

- *When* <u>you</u> <u>finish</u> this inspection, <u>we</u> <u>will prepare</u> our report.
- *Because* <u>we</u> <u>completed</u> the job on time and without errors, <u>XYZ Company</u> <u>has signed</u> a new contract for our services.
- <u>Jamir</u> <u>will direct</u> this project *because* <u>he</u> <u>has</u> the most experience with the product.

ACTIVITY 2.8

Directions: Underline each subject once. Underline the verb that goes with the subject twice. Insert the understood subject you *in sentences that are commands.*

1. The lead engineer develops the software for our department.

2. The supervisor and the team members test the new procedures.

3. Glenda Hanson directs this service project, and we are planning to review the progress on March 1.

4. Press the Manual Feed button.

5. The clerks filling, labeling, and stacking cartons to meet the inspection requirements of the manufacturing standards.

COMMON SUBJECT AND VERB AGREEMENT ERRORS

This section explains how to avoid several common (and serious) errors in subject and verb agreement. These errors diminish your professional image.

RULE 1 — A singular subject requires a singular verb.

- <u>Carlos</u> <u>is</u> an accountant.

RULE 2 — A plural subject requires a plural verb.

- The <u>accountants</u> <u>are</u> working on this project.

- <u>Carlos and Alisa</u> <u>are</u> accountants.

RULE 3 — The following subjects are singular and require singular verbs:

> each   one   every

- <u>Each</u> of the letters and memos <u>is</u> signed.

- <u>One</u> of the reports about accidents and thefts <u>is</u> missing.

- <u>Every one</u> of the assistants and file clerks <u>has</u> had the training.

RULE 4 — A singular subject described by plural words requires a singular verb to agree with the singular subject.

In the examples below, the modifying or describing words are placed in parentheses.

- The <u>package</u> (of receipt books and ledger forms) <u>was received</u> yesterday. *Package* is the singular subject. The words *of receipt books and ledger forms* describe the subject, *package*. Therefore, the verb, *was received*, must be singular to agree with the subject, *package*.

- The <u>report</u> (about many security leaks and infringements) <u>is</u> missing.

 TIP   *Ask yourself what you can remove from the sentence and still have a complete thought.*

ACTIVITY 2.9

Directions: Place parentheses around the modifying words, and underscore the true subject. Now see how easy it is to determine whether the verb should be singular or plural based on the true subject of the sentence.

1. The display of our computerized courseware selections and textbooks (is, are) well designed.

2. The large office located near our sales training rooms (is, are) reserved for sales directors.

RULE 5 — One gerund used as the subject is always singular. The verb must also be singular even if it is modified by one or more plural expressions.

- <u>*Writing*</u> reports, documentaries, and sales proposals <u>is</u> my job.

- <u>*Completing*</u> the research, the development, and the three evaluations <u>is</u> our current priority.

RULE 6 — When two or more gerunds are used as the subject, the verb must be plural to agree.

- <u>*Developing*</u> (instructional programs) and <u>*presenting*</u> (the instruction) (is, <u>are</u>) my specialties.

ACTIVITY 2.10

Directions: Circle the correct verb form in the following sentences.

1. Marissa Jones and Brandin Hayes (was, were) in the same graduating class.

2. Each of the regional proposals and sales reports (is, are) to be signed by the director.

3. Every one of the supervisors and managers (have, has) been informed of the policy.

4. One of the packages of pens, pencils, and tablets (are, is) on my desk.

5. Preparing the inventory reports and daily invoices accurately (is, are) essential to our success.

6. The order for textbooks, printers, computers, and diskettes (is, are) ready for delivery.

7. Producing a quality product and marketing it effectively (is, are) vital for us to maintain our competitive position.

PROOF POINT!

Directions: On the line next to each item, write C if the item is a complete sentence and I if the item is an incomplete sentence. Also mark revisions required to correct any errors in subject and verb agreement.

_____ 1. Because they have completed the entire project ahead of schedule and without any budget overruns.

_____ 2. Developing the new model to review in detail before starting initial production.

_____ 3. The new group of physical therapists and trainers are located on the first floor of this building.

_____ 4. In the past, each of the sales contest winners were awarded an all-expenses-paid vacation to Hawaii.

_____ 5. Of course, writing clear letters, e-mail messages, and reports are highly important.

Power Tools for Emphasis and Conciseness

Objectives

After completing Chapter 3, you will be able to:

- Use active and passive voice to your advantage.
- Eliminate dummy subjects.
- Eliminate camouflaged and weak verbs.

ACTIVE AND PASSIVE VOICE

The term *voice* refers to the relationship of the subject and its verb. In the active voice, the subject acts or performs the action. (The subject is the doer.) In the passive voice, the subject is acted upon or receives the action. (The subject is not the doer of the action.)

Active Voice

In the active voice, the subject is the doer of the action.

- <u>She</u> <u>wrote</u> the report.

  (The subject, *she,* performs the main action and is positioned directly before the verb to emphasize clearly who is performing the action.)

Passive Voice

In the passive voice, the subject is *not* the doer of the action.

- The <u>report</u> <u>was written</u> by him.

  (The subject, *report,* is not the doer of the action. The relationship of the doer to the action is not as clear because the doer, *him,* is not placed directly before the verb. In fact, it is separated from and follows the verb, reducing the readability.)

 TIP

Structure your writing to emphasize or de-emphasize by using active or passive voice to your advantage. This increases your ability to achieve the reader impact you desire.

Use of Active and Passive

Readability experts agree that active voice is usually the best choice because it is easier to comprehend than passive voice. The relationship between subject and verb is clearer in the active voice, which adds force and momentum to a message. However, some messages are communicated better in the passive voice. The individual uses and benefits of both the active and the passive voice are explained below.

The active voice has vigor. Writers often use passive voice when active voice would serve their needs better. The active voice uses a clearly identified doer of the action. This style is easy to read, is shorter, and is more interesting to read because it emphasizes people rather than objects. The active voice is preferable for emphasizing or drawing attention to the doer in a positive situation.

CONCEPT REVIEW

USES AND BENEFITS OF ACTIVE VOICE

(Emphasizes the doer of the action)

1. Emphasis on the doer of the action

2. More concise

3. Increased clarity

4. Easier to read

5. More interesting

The passive voice is preferable in some cases, and good writers use it to advantage to communicate some types of messages. The passive voice serves to de-emphasize rather than emphasize. It typically emphasizes the object rather than the doer of the action. The passive voice must be used when the doer is unknown because in the active voice, the subject is the doer of the action. Passive voice can be useful when you want to soften the effect of bad news, de-emphasize poor performance, or de-emphasize a negative situation. The passive voice is also used to add variety when the active voice has been used too repetitively.

CONCEPT REVIEW

USES AND BENEFITS OF PASSIVE VOICE

(De-emphasizes the doer of the action)

1. To de-emphasize the doer of negative action

2. To emphasize the object, not the doer

3. To break up repetitive use of active voice

4. To present content when the doer is unimportant or unknown

---

ACTIVITY 3.1

Directions: Read the active and passive examples, and discuss these questions:

1. Under what circumstances would it be preferable to use the active voice example?

2. When would it be preferable to use the passive voice example?

Active: The <u>bank</u> <u>raised</u> the interest rates today. (The subject, *bank,* is the doer of the action, *raised.*)

Passive: The <u>interest</u> rates <u>were raised</u> today. (The subject, *interest rates,* receives the action, *were raised.* The doer is not identified.)

Active or passive? Your objective determines the choice. In some cases, you will want to emphasize the doer of the action; in others, you will want to emphasize the object receiving the action. Study the following examples:

   Active: The <u>accountants</u> <u>compute</u> the totals.

   Passive: The <u>totals</u> <u>are computed</u> by the accountants.

In the active voice example, the emphasis is placed on the people who computed the totals (the accountants). In the passive voice example, the emphasis is placed on the totals, not on the people who computed them. Both constructions are grammatically correct.

ACTIVITY 3.2

Directions: Compare the following examples. Discuss under what circumstances you would choose one over the other.

   Passive: The <u>best seller</u> *In Search of Excellence* <u>was written</u> by Thomas Peters.

   Active: <u>Thomas Peters</u> <u>wrote</u> the best seller *In Search of Excellence.*

Your answer depends on your objective. If *you* wrote the prize-winning novel, which construction would you prefer? (The active voice would place the focus on you, the writer; and it would be a more lively style.) If you were a reporter writing an article to emphasize this best-selling book, which construction would you use? (The passive style emphasizes the book—the better choice for this purpose.)

Passive to Active Construction

When you want to revise a cumbersome passive construction and write it in the active voice, use these three easy steps to analyze and revise the sentence:

1. Locate the main verb in the sentence.

2. Determine who or what is doing the action of the main verb.

3. Make the doer of the action the subject of the verb, whether the doer is identified in the original sentence or not.

> *Example:*   Maintenance of electronic equipment is monitored by area supervisors.
>
> *Revision:*   1. main verb = monitored
>
>   2. doer of action = supervisors
>
>   3. revision = Area supervisors monitor maintenance of electronic equipment.

ACTIVITY 3.3

Directions: Apply the three-step analysis technique to revise the following sentence.

The tubes are tested in a sterile environment by our engineers.

1. Main verb: _____

2. Doer of action: _____

3. Revision: _____

ACTIVITY 3.4

Directions: Examine documents you have written previously. Do you tend to write predominately in one voice or another? Are you using voice to emphasize and de-emphasize effectively depending on the situation? Are you shifting from one voice to another in the same sentence? Ideally, you should use the same voice within a sentence although you can shift voice within a paragraph.

DUMMY SUBJECTS

The **dummy subject** incorporates *it* or *there* and some form of the verb *to be* at the beginning of a sentence. This weak construction is not a true subject and adds unnecessary wording. Eliminate this pattern by making the doer of the action the subject.

> *No:*   There are several good applicants who have applied.
>
> *Yes:*   Several good applicants have applied.

ACTIVITY 3.5

Directions: Revise the following sentences to eliminate the dummy subjects.

1. It is my job to prepare the final audit reports.

2. There was a demonstration of the equipment by Ms. Gonzales.

3. It is required for us to inspect the product at three points during production.

ACTIVITY 3.6

Part A
Directions: Rewrite using the active voice.

1. An outstanding presentation is always given by Dr. Franklin.

_____

Part B
Directions: Rewrite using the passive voice.

2. We have raised your annual premium by 2 percent to compensate for the new tax laws.

_____

3. Our sales representative, Don Zhao, quoted the price of the computer incorrectly.

_____

Part C
Directions: Rewrite to eliminate the dummy subject.

4. There are five projects we must complete by October 30.

_____

CAMOUFLAGED AND WEAK VERBS

A *camouflaged verb* is one that conceals or buries a stronger core verb. Replace camouflaged verbs with specific verbs that have more energy and clarity and that capture the essence of the action. Use verbs that describe actions all by themselves without helping words or phrases.

ACTIVITY 3.7

Directions: Provide a stronger verb for each camouflaged verb listed below.

Camouflaged	Better
1. make substitution	substitute
2. have intention	
3. make a decision	
4. was becoming	
5. offer a suggestion	
6. made a recommendation to	
7. gave assistance	
8. was responsible for supervision of	
9. conducted an inspection of	
10. did the marketing for	

 CONCEPT REVIEW

REVIEW THE FOLLOWING EXAMPLES

Note how use of active voice and elimination of dummy subjects and camouflaged verbs enhance conciseness and how camouflaged and passive verb constructions add unnecessary excess wording.

Dummy Subject, Camouflaged, Passive:	There was a demonstration of the procedures given by the trainer. (11 words)
Active and Camouflaged:	The trainer gave a demonstration of the procedure. (8 words)
Passive:	The procedure was demonstrated by the trainer. (7 words)
Active:	The trainer demonstrated the procedure. (5 words)

PROOF POINT!

Directions: Follow these steps to check your understanding of the concepts presented in the chapter.

1. Circle the doer of the action in each of the sentences below. (In some cases, the doer is not mentioned.)

2. Classify each of the sentences by circling *A* for active, *P* for passive, and *D* for dummy subject construction. Circle *A* and *P* if the sentence shifts from one voice to the other.

3. Underline any camouflaged verbs.

A/P/D   a.   The purchasing department processed our invoices.

A/P/D   b.   There was a hybrid corn developed in North America by our researchers.

A/P/D   c.   We completed the research on time, and the results were mailed today.

A/P/D   d.   The accountants did an audit of the business operations for the last three quarters.

A/P/D   e.   The decision had already been made by the committee.

CHAPTER**4**

Punctuation Essentials

Objectives

After completing Chapter 4, you will be able to:

- Use essential rules of the comma correctly.
- Use essential rules of the colon correctly.
- Use essential rules of the semicolon correctly.

USE OF THE COMMA

The comma is the most frequently used (and, therefore, most frequently misused) mark of punctuation. The primary business uses of the comma are to set off introductory elements and dependent clauses at the beginning of sentences, to separate elements in a series, to separate independent clauses joined by a coordinating conjunction, and to separate reversible adjectives.

RULE 1 — Use a comma after an introductory word or phrase.

- Considering the number of complaints, we plan to revise our claims processing procedures.
- To record your message, press the REC button.
- No, I cannot attend the meeting on May 8.

RULE 2 — Use a comma to separate a dependent clause (one that cannot stand by itself as a complete thought) from an independent clause when the dependent clause comes first. Place the comma after the dependent clause.

Dependent clauses usually begin with one of the following words: *if, when, since, because, after, before, although, as, while, unless,* and *until.*

- When he finishes high school, he plans to go to the university.

RULE 3 — Use a comma to separate words, phrases, or clauses listed in a series.

- The agenda items include the following: budgets, training, and advertising. (words)
- Our goals are to complete the research, to analyze the data, and to compile a final report. (phrases)

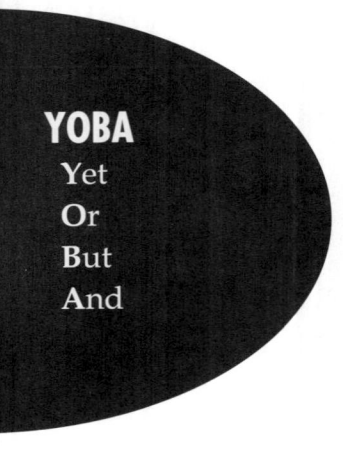

YOBA
Yet
Or
But
And

- Jan will prepare the brochure, Max will handle registration, and I will coordinate the speakers. (clauses)

RULE 4 — Use a comma in a compound sentence before a coordinating conjunction: *yet*, *or*, *but*, and *and*. (Remember the acronym shown at the left.)

- He is writing a book, and she is studying law.
- He worked as an assistant for three years, and he has just been promoted to general manager.
- Call Pat Oki to confirm our meeting, and make flight reservations to San Diego.

RULE 5 — Use a comma to separate two or more adjectives that are reversible.

- The team prepared a thorough, effective presentation.
- This is a useful, interesting, dynamic workshop.

ACTIVITY 4.1

Directions: Insert commas where they are needed in the following sentences.

1. He presented an organized persuasive proposal to our central planning committee.

2. If Michi succeeds in this course she will receive a certificate.

3. In the rush of excitement he overlooked an important detail.

4. We will collect information from all departments and the appointed representatives will make the final decision.

5. Mike is going to the conference but Jacinta has another obligation.

6. Please add the following classes to our community education brochure: Spanish I, computerized bookkeeping, defensive driving and interviewing techniques.

USE OF THE COLON

The primary business uses of the colon are to introduce a list, to follow a salutation in a business letter, to introduce a long quotation, to separate hours and minutes in reference to time, and to separate reference initials.

RULE 1 — Use a colon before items that are listed, whether they are listed as straight text material or keyed with one item on each line. Items may or may not be numbered. Introduce the list with some form of the word *follow* (*the following*, *as follows*). Place the colon directly before the list.

- He packed the following gear: camera, flash unit, film, and tripod.
- The lecture will emphasize the following items:
  - Sentence structure
  - Subject and verb agreement
  - Parts of speech
- The winners are as follows: Jack Sharkey, Monte Levitt, and Barbara Iverson.

RULE 2 — Space once or twice after the colon except in reference initials and time of day.

- jl:st
- 2:30 p.m.

RULE 3 — Use a colon to introduce a long direct quotation.

- He recited the entire paragraph: "The committee deliberated. . . ."

RULE 4 — Use a colon after the salutation of a business letter.

- Dear Ms. Seroski:
- Dear Mr. Townsend:

USE OF THE SEMICOLON

The primary business uses of the semicolon are to join independent clauses in the circumstances outlined below and to separate items in a series when the items contain commas.

RULE 1 — Use a semicolon to separate independent clauses of a compound sentence when the conjunction (*yet, or, but,* and *and*) is omitted.

- He took a long walk; the exercise failed to relax him.

Remember, however, that a comma is required at the end of the first clause when two independent clauses are joined by a coordinating conjunction.

- He took a long walk, but the exercise failed to relax him.

RULE 2 — Use a semicolon before a conjunctive adverb or transitional expression (a "bigger word") joining two independent clauses. (Examples of these transitional expressions are *therefore, however, consequently, accordingly, furthermore, in addition, in fact, likewise, moreover, nevertheless, still, thus,* and *so.*)
Use a comma after the "bigger word."

- The logic is sound; therefore, we must accept the conclusion.

RULE 3 — Use a semicolon to separate a series of items when the items themselves contain commas. This clearly indicates the main divisions between items in the series.

- The following people were elected as our officers: Miles Nelson, president; Teri Chen, vice president; and Kate Jensen, secretary.
- Chris was selected Volunteer of the Year based on his helpful, empathetic attitude; dependability; patience; and enthusiasm.

RULE 4 — Use a semicolon in a compound sentence if either clause contains one or more commas. Place the semicolon before the conjunction ("little word") that joins the clauses.

- He took a long, brisk walk; but the exercise failed to relax him.

 TIP   *Semicolons can usually be replaced with periods. With the exception of Rule 3 above, a period can usually replace a semicolon if the semicolon is used correctly.*

 CONCEPT REVIEW

REVIEW GRAMMATICAL PATTERNS AND PUNCTUATION

Punctuation is determined by the pattern or arrangement of phrases and clauses in a sentence. Reviewing the following simple patterns will help you use punctuation correctly.

Pattern 1: Two independent clauses written as two simple sentences

- Brent took a long walk. The exercise relaxed him.

Pattern 2: Two independent clauses joined by a semicolon

- Brent took a long walk; the exercise relaxed him.

Pattern 3: Two independent clauses joined by a conjunction, "little word" (a comma is placed before the "little word")

- Brent took a long walk, and the exercise relaxed him.

Pattern 4: Two independent clauses joined by a "bigger word" (a semicolon is placed before and a comma is placed after the "bigger word")

- Lydia prepared well; therefore, she gave an exceptional speech.

Pattern 5: One dependent clause, a comma, one independent clause

- Because she prepared well, Lydia gave an exceptional speech. ("flag word")

Pattern 6: One introductory phrase, a comma, and one independent clause

- According to the report, we have increased sales by 20 percent this year.

PROOF POINT!

Directions: Insert commas, colons, and semicolons where needed.

1. Because he has been with the company for one year he is eligible for the following benefits dental medical profit sharing and retirement fund.

2. To complete the application for copyright follow the instructions in the enclosed booklet.

3. Davis is heading the marketing division Teresita is in charge of manufacturing

4. We will attend the conference in Dallas but I will be leaving early to travel to Atlanta for a sales meeting.

5. He is qualified to give the presentation however he will not be available that day.

6. We have red, black, and green pens but we suggest using the black pens on transparencies.

7. The questionnaire results are not yet in consequently we will have to delay our final report.

8. He presented an exciting detailed description of the event.

CHAPTER 5

Power Tools for Balance and Clarity

Objectives

After completing Chapter 5, you will be able to:

- Use parallel structure.
- Place modifiers correctly.
- Use clear pronoun references.
- Avoid "stacks of nouns."

USE PARALLEL STRUCTURE

Parallel structure clarifies meaning, is grammatically correct, and is easy to read. To make a sentence parallel (*parallel* means "alike or matching"), ideas of equal importance are constructed alike using the same grammatical form. This structural similarity creates a balance that helps the reader understand the relationship of the ideas.

Assume you want to list three actions for your reader to take. Express each one in the same grammatical form—all verbs, all nouns, all phrases, or all gerunds. Don't mix grammatical forms.

Notice in the last example below how the shift in grammatical form requires the reader to shift structural gears in translating the message. The result is unclear writing.

Yes: **Read** the contract, **sign** it with your full legal name, and **return** it to us within ten days. (All three actions are written with a verb expressing a simple command.)

No: **Read** the contract, **sign** it with your full legal name, and **we should receive** it from you within ten days. (The first two actions are expressed with verbs in the simple command form; the last action is constructed as a statement.)

Using parallel structure in the first draft of a communication is not essential, as the goal of a first draft is to roughly expand on key concepts. However, using parallel structure throughout the final document is required for developing clear, professional content.

RULE 1 — Balance grammatical usage in sentences (words, parts of speech, clauses, and sentences within a paragraph).

Use nouns with nouns.

No: I like **tennis, archery,** and **to play chess.** (Incorrect: The first two elements are nouns, and the third element is an infinitive.)

Yes: I like **tennis, archery,** and **chess.** (Correct: All three elements are nouns.)

Use gerunds with gerunds (*ing* with *ing*).

No: **Writing** the proposal is important, but **to present** it is equally critical to our success. (A gerund is used with an infinitive.)

Yes: **Writing** the proposal is important, but **presenting** it is equally critical to our success. (A gerund is used with a gerund.)

Use adjectives with adjectives.

No: Ronaldo is **intelligent, reliable**, and **has** an outgoing personality. (The first two elements are adjectives, and the last element is a verb.)

Yes: Ronaldo is **intelligent, reliable**, and **outgoing**. (All three elements are adjectives.)

Use infinitives with infinitives, *to* + *verb* (*to* with *to*).

No: Dorian plans **to go** to the workshop, **to meet** with the speaker, and she **will discuss** her proposal with him. (The first two elements are infinitives; the last element is a verb.)

Yes: Dorian plans **to go** to the workshop, **to meet** with the speaker, and **to discuss** her proposal with him. (All three elements are infinitives.)

Use verbs with verbs.

No: He **works** quickly, **follows** proper safety procedures, and **with** excellent attention to detail. (The first two elements are verbs, but the last element is a preposition.)

Yes: He **works** quickly, **follows** proper safety procedures, and **performs** with excellent attention to detail. (All three elements are verbs—*works, follows, performs.*)

RULE 2 — To achieve parallelism, repeat an article (*the, a, an*), repeat an infinitive (*to* plus the verb—as in *to walk*), repeat a preposition (*at, in, for, by, from*), or repeat the introductory word of a long clause or phrase.

Repeat a preposition.

No: The success of the crops was influenced **by** natural factors such as rainfall and insect infestations and the availability of farm laborers. (The first element is introduced by a preposition; the second is not.)

Yes: The success of the crops was influenced **by** natural factors such as rainfall and insect infestations and **by** the availability of farm laborers. (The preposition *by* is used with each element, balancing the message.)

ACTIVITY 5.1

Part A
Directions: Correct all errors in parallel construction by writing in the necessary revisions.

1. Our goals are to expand the sales force, to increase our regional offices, and increasing company profits by 25 percent.

2. He is responsible for scheduling the construction projects and to meet all safety requirements.

3. We will discuss our budget plans for cross-training operators and two more laptop computers.

4. The speaker covered the topic well, used appropriate visual aids, and within the time allotted.

Part B
Directions: Revise the following list to make it parallel.

1. Plans to remodel the regional office.

2. Increasing the advertising budget.

3. We will hire two new sales representatives.

4. Schedule software training for all staff.

 TIP *All items in a list should be complete sentences or phrases—not a mix of the two. Whenever possible, use phrases instead of sentences to achieve conciseness. Begin each phrase with the same part of speech to achieve parallelism in the list.*

PLACE MODIFIERS CORRECTLY

A **modifier** is a word or phrase used to describe. Take care to place modifiers correctly to assure that they modify the proper word or words and that they convey the desired meaning. Misplacement of modifiers often confuses or amuses your reader and may distort your actual intent.

RULE 1 — Place modifying words or phrases as close as possible to the words they describe.

> *No:* **Lying on the cabinet, you** will find the Weston file. (It sounds as though you have to lie on the cabinet to find the file.)

> *Yes:* You will find the Weston **file lying** on the cabinet.

RULE 2 — If necessary, repeat the subject for clarity.

> *No:* **I** saw the auditorium walking through the hotel.

> *Yes:* As **I** was walking through the hotel, **I** saw the auditorium.

RULE 3 — Place frequently misplaced adverbs as close as possible to the words they modify.

almost	hardly	merely	only
even	just	nearly	scarcely

Notice how modifier placement changes the meaning in the following sentences.

1. I **only asked** for two copies. (and nothing else)

2. I asked for **only two copies.** (not three, not four)

3. **Only I** asked for two copies. (not you, *I* asked for more)

4. I **nearly dropped all** of the reports. (almost dropped but didn't)

5. I **dropped nearly all** of the reports. (did drop reports)

ACTIVITY 5.2

Directions: Mark each sentence to indicate where the modifiers should be moved to achieve maximum clarity.

1. In this report, there are many references to illegal accounting practices, which the senior accounting manager has recommended for the staff.

2. If your facsimile machine breaks down within 24 hours, it will be repaired free of charge.

3. When you return from travel, you should submit your reimbursement request with receipts attached to your supervisor.

USE CLEAR PRONOUN REFERENCES

An **antecedent** is a word or group of words to which a pronoun refers. The pronoun must agree with its antecedent in number and gender (male or female). Pronouns must also clearly reference their antecedents.

Make Pronouns Agree in Number and Gender

A pronoun must agree with its antecedent in number. If the antecedent is singular, the pronoun must be singular. If the antecedent is plural, the pronoun must be plural. A pronoun must also match the gender of its antecedent. The following pronouns and the words they refer to agree in number and gender (male or female).

- **Mr. Redding** gave **his** presentation at 8 p.m.
  (The antecedent, *Mr. Redding*, is the word referred to by the pronoun, *his*. The pronoun, *his*, and the antecedent, *Mr. Redding*, are both singular and masculine.)

- The **engineers and the technicians** presented **their** views.
  (The antecedent, *engineers* and *technicians*, and the pronoun referencing it, *their*, are both plural and neutral in gender.)

ACTIVITY 5.3

Directions: Correct the errors in agreement in the following sentences.

1. That company is expanding their product line rapidly.

2. Each employee is required to sign their time cards.

3. Every member of the league of insurance women had their copy of the proposal.

Make Certain Pronouns Clearly Reference Antecedents

Proofread and revise your writing as necessary to correct any unclear pronoun references. This occurs when the pronoun does not clearly indicate the antecedent (the word to which the pronoun refers).

Unclear: The supervisor told the employee that **he** should return at 4 p.m. (Who should return—the supervisor or the employee? The pronoun, *he*, doesn't clarify which word is the correct antecedent—*supervisor* or *employee*.)

Clear: The supervisor told the employee to return at 4 p.m.

ACTIVITY 5.4

Directions: Mark the required correction to achieve clarity of pronoun reference in the following sentence.

Complete the illustration and the statistical chart, and give it to our production department this afternoon.

AVOID "STACKS OF NOUNS"

A "stack of nouns" occurs when a sentence contains too many consecutive nouns or modifying nouns. One way to enhance clarity is to edit "stacks of nouns" so you have no more than three in a row. Correcting "stacks of nouns" is easy to do, and it improves the clarity of the message. Follow the guidelines below to correct this error:

1. Edit consecutive strings of more than three modifying nouns.

2. Whenever possible, limit the number of consecutive modifying nouns to two.

3. Where appropriate, use a preposition to break up too many consecutive nouns. (See the sample prepositions below.)

above	beside	from	on	toward
at	between	in	over	under
behind	by	of	past	upon
below	for	off	to	with

Notice in the first example below how the stack of consecutive modifying nouns is difficult to read. Also notice how the revision enhances clarity by eliminating one of the noun constructions, by spreading the others throughout the sentence, and by using the preposition *in* to break up the stack.

Poor: We specialize in **resource management systems development training.**
(5 modifying nouns in a row)

Better: Our **specialty** is developmental **training** *in* **resource management.**
(2 modifying nouns in a row)

ACTIVITY 5.5

Directions: Revise the following draft to eliminate the stack of modifying nouns.

He presented the report highlighting their waste disposal systems policy development strategies.

_____

_____

_____

_____

_____

PROOF POINT!

Directions: In the following letter, circle and label all of the errors and write in suggested improvements. Look for these errors:

Throughout: use of commas

Paragraph 1: active/passive voice   stack of nouns   camouflaged verb

Paragraph 2: dummy subject   parallel structure

Paragraph 3: camouflaged verb

Paragraph 4: camouflaged verb   pronoun reference error

June 2, 200-

Rico Cortez, Vice President
Rathwell, Inc.
1400 Landon Way
Portland, OR 97207

Dear Mr. Cortez:

BUDGET PRIORITIES ASSESSMENT

The annual sales budget priorities assessment you recently asked me to develop has been completed, and a report has been prepared for the board of directors. The recommendations were determined with attention to priority and I have also given careful consideration to cost effectiveness. A copy of the report is enclosed.

There are three items that have been emphasized in this report and they are as follows: to increase computer applications training, to update marketing catalogs, and expanding office space.

All of our team members completed the departmental needs survey and I used this data to put together a compilation report of their responses. As you can see in this report the majority of team members rated the need for computer applications training as a top budgetary priority.

Because training in computer applications was rated as a top priority I am making the recommendation that we approve funding for them early in the new fiscal year.

Sincerely,

Sondra Whiting

rlm

Enclosure

CHAPTER 6

Custom Tools to Persuade Readers

Objectives

After completing Chapter 6, you will be able to:

- Focus on the needs of your reader.
- Write in a positive tone.

NEEDS OF THE READER

Effective writing focuses on the reader because readers respond most favorably to messages that reflect their own needs, not just those of the writer. In addition to focusing on the reader's needs, you will be most persuasive if you write in a positive tone. People are instinctively drawn toward positive words; they also are instinctively repelled by a negative tone.

TIP *Attract your reader's attention to get the results you want. You can boost the likelihood of getting the reader reaction you want by writing messages that:*

- Reflect the reader's needs and interests.
- Make the reader feel important.
- Use a positive tone.
- Aim to show benefits for the reader.

ACTIVITY 6.1

Directions: Read the three letters your instructor displays on slides. Assume the letters were written to you. (You have applied to serve as a reading tutor and are enthused about the possibility of being involved in the state literacy program.) Which message do you like best? Why? Which one makes you feel most important? Why?

Use the *You Emphasis*

Many writers focus on achieving their own objectives—certainly an important reason for writing. But when the needs and interests of the reader are not addressed, the outcome is

39

often unsuccessful. The best business messages address the needs of the writer but also incorporate the *you emphasis*, meaning they reflect the needs and interests of the reader.

Motivate by emphasizing benefits for the reader — include a *WIFM*. The acronym *WIFM* stands for "What's In It For Me"—from the reader's perspective. A *WIFM* is a benefit that attracts reader attention and motivates the reader to act. Whenever your message includes a benefit for the reader or the reader's organization, present this benefit (or *WIFM*) in the first paragraph. To identify potential benefits to the reader, consider what the reader needs, wants, or expects.

Visualize and align with your reader. The most effective message is carefully designed to fit the reader. Practice visualizing the reader, using the *you emphasis*. Project empathy with your reader by thinking of and conveying your message in a style appropriate for the reader and in terms of what the reader wants or needs to know. To target your message, answer the following questions before you get started:

1. Who is the reader? Identify his or her:

   a. Business role.

   b. Approximate age.

   c. Level of education.

   d. Personality type and general values.

   e. Experience related to the topic of your message.

2. How much information does the reader need?

You may not know the reader's personality type or general values, but you should have a fair idea about the other information. If your communication is extremely important, make an effort to learn everything you can about all of the questions above. The more closely your message aligns with the reader's background and style, the more effective it will be.

Use *you, your.* You can convey empathy and encourage reader affiliation with your message by expanding the *you emphasis* to focus on *you* and *your*. The reader interprets *you* as *I* (creating the most effective emphasis—on the reader). Have you ever noticed how many advertisements capitalize on this precept? They use *you* and *your* in combination with positive aspects of their products so readers will interpret the product claim from their perspective. Notice how this works in the following example:

Example:	When **you** use *Golden Youth Drops*, **you'll** experience a 20 percent reduction in the appearance of fine lines and wrinkles.
Reader Interpretation:	When **I** use *Golden Youth Drops*, **I** will experience. . . .

On the other hand, the reader interprets *I* or *we* as *you* (creating emphasis on the writer). Compare the following examples illustrating this concept:

I/we Emphasis:	Before **we** can finalize your order, **we** must have the code numbers for the items you want.
You Emphasis:	So **you** can receive your order promptly and accurately, please write in the code numbers for the merchandise **you** want. A copy of your original order is provided for this purpose. Thank you.

ACTIVITY 6.2

Directions: Rewrite the following statement using the you *emphasis.*

This is to announce to the public that XYZ Bank is now offering expanded drive-up banking services. Our drive- up window will be open from 7:30 a.m. to 6:30 p.m. Monday through Friday.

Simply using the words *you* and *your* and avoiding the words *I* and *we* does not automatically convey a *you emphasis*. Readers can sense whether a communication projects sincerity and understanding. For the *you emphasis* to sound sincere, it must be sincere, not manipulative.

 TIP **Keep references to you** *positive.* **Use you** *in connection with positive, not negative, terms.*

Compare the following two examples. Notice that the first example contains three *you's* and two *yours* but fails to convey the *you emphasis*. The second example contains four *I's* and only two *you's* but does convey the *you emphasis*.

- You failed to supply complete information in your order; therefore, you cannot expect to have your computers when you want them.

- I'm sorry the computers could not be shipped at once. Because I wanted to make sure you received exactly what you need, I held up the order until I could get more precise information.

Be personal. Include a personal reference when appropriate: "I enjoyed talking with you." "It was certainly a pleasure meeting you." "I look forward to working with you, Pio."

Be empathetic. When appropriate, convey empathy for the reader's situation: "I would be concerned, too." "You're dealing with a difficult situation, and I'll do my best to help." "This must be stressful for you, so I'll do everything I can to speed the process."

Give your reader the complete picture. Consider how much knowledge your reader has of your subject. Approach your writing as if your reader has no knowledge of the subject, taking care to clarify ambiguous content. Remember to use terms and details that are familiar to the reader. Include all necessary information. This approach helps eliminate the need for additional clarifying communication before your reader can take appropriate action.

Consider the importance of timing. Ask yourself if now is the best time to send your reader this communication. Is this the busiest month of the year for his or her organization? If so, your reader may have more pressing priorities that could diminish the impact of your communication.

If your purpose is to make a request of your reader and you know this is a demanding time for him or her, wait to send your correspondence until the timing is better.

If the response to your correspondence is critical, time the delivery so it arrives on days other than Monday or Friday. On Mondays, businesses are usually striving to get back into the fast-paced rhythm of work. On Fridays, many people are focusing on the coming weekend.

ACTIVITY 6.3

Directions: Assume you are writing to persuade customers to schedule a meeting with you to discuss your new products or services. You have built good relationships with these people. Your objective is clear: You want to open the door for more sales. If you convey this purpose only, your chances of getting the reaction you want (a meeting with the customer) are significantly less than if you focus on the benefit to the customer. Below is the first draft of the notice you will be sending to your customers. Consider these two questions:
(1) Whose needs are emphasized in the draft? (2) When revising to meet the reader's needs, what specific WIFM or reader benefit could you emphasize first? Hint: The draft is not specific enough.

I want to meet with you to tell you about our new office products. I know you'll be especially impressed with our new customer database program *Customer Base Optima*. I'll call you next week to set up a meeting.

POSITIVE TONE—A KEY FACTOR

Express everything you write in the most positive terms possible (whether the message is positive, negative, or neutral). Readers respond most favorably to positive writing.

Tone is one of the most influential keys to writing success, and you can control the tone you convey. Focus on making your messages thoughtful, rather than writing in a style that is mechanical, indifferent, accusatory, negative, or curt. To help achieve a positive tone, imagine you are writing to someone you like and admire. This will help you choose persuasive and positive words. Enhance your communications success by choosing words that are considerate, friendly, and positive.

Eliminate the Negative

Avoid inadvertently using negative terms without considering the impact on the reader. With a little effort, you can usually rephrase a negative statement to make it more appealing to the reader.

You can soften negative messages by choosing words carefully. You can even make a severe reprimand less painful by including constructive suggestions for improvement and by offering assistance where appropriate. Making this extra effort increases chances that your writing will result in the action you want.

Avoid expressions that have a negative connotation, such as these:

but	don't	I'll try	never
cannot	failure	impossible	no
difficult	however	neglected	regret

Avoid words that convey distasteful feelings or thoughts.

cheap	expensive	painful	stench
disgusting	mushy	putrid	sweaty

ACTIVITY 6.4

Directions: Circle the word in each group that conveys the most positive tone.

1. skinny   scrawny   slender

2. responsibility   chore   challenge

3. recognized   honored   commended

Emphasize what you *can* do, not what you *can't* do.

No: We cannot fill your order until October 15.

Yes: Thank you for your order. It will be shipped to you on October 15.

Be courteous and avoid a demanding or demoralizing tone. Address real problems, but don't use demoralizing descriptors. People don't like to be commanded; they prefer to be asked and to be given reasons. Compare these two columns. The words in the left column that convey a negative tone are in bold.

You **must**	Will you please?
We **expect** you to	Please
Return it **no later** than June 4.	Please return it by June 4.
No smoking	Smoke-free environment
Your **careless** error	Your error

When giving precautionary instructions, state the reason first. Follow the reason with an instruction of what *to* do, not a command emphasizing what *not* to do.

No: Don't forget to wear safety goggles when mixing these chemicals.

Yes: To prevent injury to your eyes, always wear safety goggles when mixing these chemicals.

Personalize Form Documents

To increase productivity, develop form documents for routine, repetitive messages. However, to convey a personal tone, customize the documents as much as possible for each receiver. Avoid canned expressions and overuse of the receiver's name—practices that smack of the impersonal form letter.

 CONCEPT REVIEW

TO ACHIEVE A POSITIVE TONE IN YOUR WRITING AND TO GET POSITIVE RESULTS:

1. Emphasize benefits to the reader (*WIFM*).

2. Avoid negative expressions.

3. Use courteous terms.

4. Use *you* and *your* to express positive content you want to emphasize.

5. Don't use *you* and *your* to point out a reader's errors or to disagree with the reader.

6. Emphasize what you *can* do, not what you *can't* do.

7. Express concern or empathy for the reader's viewpoint and needs.

8. Avoid a tone that is demanding or demoralizing.

ACTIVITY 6.5

Directions: Mark revisions to the following sentences to convey a positive, personal, and empathetic tone. Review the summary of positive tone writing techniques above.

1. All three copies of the contract must be signed and two copies returned to our department.

2. Never leave clients' files on your desk when you are away from the area.

3. Because your injury will prevent you from working for four weeks, you must complete this accident form for our records immediately.

4. You neglected to include your social security number; and without it, we cannot process your permit.

5. Your request doesn't make any sense.

PROOF POINT!

Directions: Follow these instructions to revise the draft below.

_____ 1. Cover up the revision following the draft.

_____ 2. Read the draft.

_____ 3. Circle all negative terms in the draft.

_____ 4. Edit the draft to indicate how you would improve the tone and address the needs of the reader more effectively.

_____ 5. Compare the revision to your own revised draft.

Notice how appealing the revised message is when the tools presented in Chapter 6 are used to improve the draft.

Draft

We regret to inform you that we cannot schedule your meeting in our clubhouse as it has already been reserved for the date you requested. We could let you use our conference room, but it seats only 60. Please call the number in our letterhead to confirm your decision.

Revision

Thank you for your room-scheduling request. Our conference room, which comfortably seats 60, is available for the date you requested (Thursday, March 18). Our clubhouse has already been reserved for that date. The conference room is entirely adequate to meet all of the conditions you specified.

I would be happy to confirm this reservation. Just call me directly at (208) 555-0110 or fax me your confirmation at (208) 555-0111. We look forward to serving your needs.

CHAPTER 7

Framing Tools

After completing Chapter 7, you will be able to:

- Write effective sentences.
- Write clearly focused paragraphs.
- Use transitions to guide your reader.

EFFECTIVE SENTENCES

This section provides guidelines to help you write complete and concise sentences and to use a variety of sentence structures to stimulate reader interest.

Earlier in this text-workbook, you developed the basic foundations for writing good sentences. The concepts include writing complete sentences; using basic punctuation; using active and passive voice; placing modifiers; using parallel structure and clear pronoun references; and avoiding dummy subjects, camouflaged verbs, and stacks of nouns. Those are some of the essential principles for producing strong sentences; expanded principles follow.

CONCEPT REVIEW

A sentence meets the following criteria:

1. Expresses a complete thought.

2. Contains at least one *independent clause*.

3. Contains both a *subject* and a *verb*. (The subject *you* may be understood in a command, as in the following example of the shortest possible complete sentence: *Go.*

What about Sentence Length?

Short sentences usually convey ideas more clearly and directly than long sentences. *The average length of a sentence should be about 15 to 20 words.* Beware of the long sentence. Long sentences can impede readability more than any other writing fault, particularly when too many ideas are presented in one sentence.

A long sentence is more effective and is, therefore, preferable when it focuses on one idea and conveys the idea more clearly than a shorter sentence.

Sentence Variety Enhances Writing Impact

To avoid monotony, incorporate a variety of sentence types (simple, compound, and complex) in your writing. Limiting yourself to one sentence type creates monotony for your reader.

CONCEPT REVIEW

SIMPLE AND COMPOUND SENTENCES

A simple sentence is an independent clause that contains one subject and one verb. Use simple sentences to emphasize an idea, but don't overuse this sentence type. If you do, your writing will be choppy and amateurish.

- <u>He</u> <u>is</u> a good speaker.
- <u>He</u> <u>lectures</u> especially well on economics.

A compound sentence contains two closely allied simple sentences joined by a coordinating conjunction (*yet, or, but,* and *and*). A comma is placed before the conjunction to indicate the end of the first thought. Use compound sentences to add variety to your writing and to help the reader understand relationships between thoughts.

- <u>He</u> <u>is</u> a good speaker, and <u>he</u> <u>lectures</u> especially well on economics.
- <u>I</u> <u>sent</u> a written proposal, and <u>I</u> <u>presented</u> it in person.

ACTIVITY 7.1

Directions: In the examples below, three related ideas are written as three simple sentences. If you received a letter written this way, what would be your reaction? Why? Rewrite this message in one concise sentence.

1. He is an attorney.

2. He specializes in corporate law.

3. He is with the firm of Haskins and Bowden.

_____

_____

CONCEPT REVIEW

COMPLEX SENTENCE

The complex sentence is composed of one independent clause (or simple sentence) and one or more dependent clauses (a clause that cannot stand alone as a sentence). Use this structure to emphasize one idea (the first one) and to express more than one idea in a sentence.

ACTIVITY 7.2

Directions: In each of the following sentences, (a) circle the subordinating conjunction or "flag word" (the word that ties the two clauses together) and (b) underline the independent clause.

- When you complete the training satisfactorily, you will receive a certificate.

- He missed his connection to Miami because the flight was late leaving Phoenix.

CLEARLY FOCUSED PARAGRAPHS

Paragraphs are used to present topics in a written communication. They are designed to group related content together and to build the message logically for the reader.

A well-written paragraph should meet the following structural criteria:

1. A paragraph consists of one or more sentences that support one main idea.

2. This main idea or purpose is expressed in the **topic sentence,** which is usually (but not always) the first sentence in the paragraph.

3. All other sentences in the paragraph should contribute to this main purpose.

4. Each paragraph logically supports the central idea, theme, or purpose of the overall communication.

Other elements of good paragraphs include the following:

Focus	The paragraph sticks to one idea and doesn't ramble.
Emphasis	The important information is placed at the beginning and/or end of the paragraph.
Organization	The content is logically structured and flows smoothly into the next paragraph.

Spark Interest with Short Paragraphs

Readers don't like wading through long, solid blocks of copy. Increase interest and readability with short paragraphs that are *about five to nine keyed* lines or that have *about three to six sentences.*

If a paragraph becomes too long, break it at a logical point, even if you're still addressing one idea. This gives your reader a visual breather. Interest and comprehension take a nosedive when your reader has to read a paragraph more than once to find or understand the main point.

Use short paragraphs so your reader can grasp the message quickly and act or respond the way you want. However, as with sentences, vary the length of paragraphs to keep your reader from getting bored.

For extra emphasis, set one sentence (or even one word) off as a paragraph—an excellent technique for focusing attention.

See?

 CONCEPT REVIEW

Use the following techniques to get your writing started:

1. Brainstorm the content of your communication by clustering your ideas freely—jotting down key ideas without analyzing to get your thoughts going. This right-brain process creates momentum for your writing.

2. Review your key ideas, add to them as necessary, and number them in logical order for effective development of your message.

3. If necessary, create a more formal outline from your cluster before drafting your message.

4. Write a quick right brain-centered draft. Expand your clustered or outlined thoughts into paragraphs.

5. Once you have written your first draft, edit it for correctness and completeness, focusing on the left-brain analytical processes.

Focus Paragraphs with Topic Sentences

Effective paragraphs have **unity;** that is, they focus on one idea (usually the theme of the topic sentence) and all sentences in the paragraph relate to that idea. Therefore, the key to writing good paragraphs is to develop specific topic ideas clearly. Avoid rambling and making the topic too broad, thereby defeating the purpose of addressing only one topic per paragraph.

The topic sentence expresses the main idea of the paragraph. The topic sentence is typically the first sentence of the paragraph (direct method of development) or the last sentence (indirect method of development).

The direct method of paragraph development provides the reader with a preview of the main idea, which aids comprehension of the paragraph. The indirect method does not state the main idea initially; it leads the reader to the main point or conclusion. This method is sometimes used to surprise the reader, as in comedy or suspense.

The ideas that emerge from your clustering are often the foundations for your paragraphs. Also ask the key questions *Who? What? Why? Where? When? How?* and *How much?* to help focus your topic sentences.

Review the following topic sentences. Note how the weak example is not focused on one idea but the better example is.

Weak: How is children's dental health improving and why?
          (Two ideas to be developed: *how* = fewer cavities; *why* = fluoride)

Better: How is children's dental health improving?
          (One idea to be developed: *how* = fewer cavities)
          (A separate paragraph should be developed to discuss *why* children's dental health is improving.)

ACTIVITY 7.3

Directions: Assume that the ad below is for your kitchen appliance repair company. The ad would run in the telephone directory. Consider which topic potential customers would look for first when searching the yellow pages for a company to repair a malfunctioning refrigerator. Respond to the items following the ad.

Draft of Ad: We offer reliable and quick service, and we are certified to repair more kitchen appliance makes and models than any of our competitors in the greater Detroit area.

1. How many topics are included in the topic sentence of the original ad?

_____

2. Based on information in the directions, write a stronger topic sentence.

_____

3. What facts could you add to support your revised topic sentence?

_____

TRANSITIONS

Transitions are linking words or expressions as well as graphics that connect ideas for the reader, increasing ease of reading and comprehension. Transitions lead the reader from sentence to sentence and from paragraph to paragraph.

Use Word Transitions to Connect Ideas

Examples of word transitions include *following, since, however, because, for example,* and *finally.* Because transitions increase the readability of your message, they increase the likelihood of getting the response you want from the reader.

 TIP *Transitions tie ideas and paragraphs to each other, connecting ideas smoothly.*

Examples of Transitional Expressions

Purpose	Transition
To add *similar information*	similarly, also, furthermore, likewise, and numbers (first, second, third, etc.)
To add *conflicting* or *contrasting* information	however, but, yet, in contrast, on the other hand, otherwise
To indicate a *list*	following, listed below
To add *examples* or explanatory information	for example, for instance, in other words, such as, likewise, similarly, specifically
To indicate *result*	therefore, consequently, as a result, because, since, thus, accordingly
To signal a *conclusion*	after all, at last, finally, in conclusion, to conclude, to summarize

To help the reader grasp a complex or technical concept:

1. Define the concept.
2. Use the transition *for example* followed by a simple example phrased in common terms.

> In dentistry, the term *lingual* means "toward the tongue." For example, a lingual cavity is located on the tongue side of the mouth as opposed to the cheek side of the mouth.

Use Headings, Font Enhancements, Lists, and Graphics

Help your reader grasp complex messages by using appropriate visual transitions.

Use headings to emphasize topics. Use centered main headings in all capital letters, side sub-headings in initial capital letters, and paragraph headings (with only the first word capitalized) to guide the reader through documents. Headings also provide a preview of upcoming content that speeds comprehension.

Use lists to clarify details. Use numbers, letters, or bullets—especially useful for making complex material more readable. Readers are better able to see each item of detail in a list and are less likely to skip items than when forced to comprehend details buried in paragraph format.

Use font enhancements for emphasis. Use bold text to emphasize headings, words, and phrases in the body of your message. Use italics to refer to specific terms.

Use graphics where appropriate. Use quality images or illustrations to add interest. Also use graphs or tables to make detailed data more readable.

Have you ever been overwhelmed by long paragraphs with no visual breathers? Solid blocks of text are instant turn-offs to readers. Provide breaks in long paragraphs by using headings, lists, and graphics.

ACTIVITY 7.4

Directions: Compare the draft below with the revision that follows. Note in the revision how the bulleted list, the headings, and the bold and italic text increase the readability of the message and how the graphic image adds interest.

Draft

Voice Qualities Impact Your Presentation

How you say the words impacts your audience enormously. Three voice characteristics influence your presentation: loudness, rate, and pitch. Speaking too loudly is almost as bad as speaking too softly. You can achieve just the right volume by aiming to speak to the people seated near the back of the room. However, variations in loudness are most effective. Dropping your voice to a whisper can be as effective as raising it to a shout. Speaking too fast for too long inhibits effective communication. On the other hand, if you talk too slowly, you may put people to sleep. The magic words are variety, change of pace, and pause. Avoid the monotony of using the same pitch. Use variations and inflections to keep your audience alert.

Revision

Note: In the example below, the word transitions, which connect ideas for the reader, are underlined.

Voice Qualities Impact Your Presentation

How you say the words impacts your audience enormously. The following three voice characteristics influence your presentation:

- Loudness

- Rate

- Pitch

Techniques for projecting effective voice qualities in public speaking <u>are explained below</u>.

Loudness

Speaking too loudly is almost as bad as speaking too softly. You can achieve just the right volume by aiming to speak to the people seated near the back of the room. However, variations in loudness are most effective. Dropping your voice to a whisper can be as effective as raising it to a shout.

Rate

To achieve peak effectiveness in oral presentations, you must also master your rate of speech. Speaking too fast for too long inhibits effective communication. On the other hand, if you talk too slowly, you may put people to sleep. The magic words are *variety, change of pace,* and *pause.*

Pitch

<u>Also</u> avoid the monotony of using the same pitch. Use variations and inflections to keep your audience alert.

ACTIVITY 7.5

Directions: Use the clustering technique to brainstorm the content of a business letter or an e-mail message—ideally one you actually need to write. Then refer to your cluster as you complete the template below. This template will help you organize your message efficiently before you begin the actual writing. Not all paragraphs require a transition or a heading—use these as appropriate.

Power Tools Template for Letters, Memos, and E-mail Messages

Introductory Paragraph

Purpose: _____

_____

WIFM: _____

_____

Transition: _____

_____

Body/Paragraph 2

Heading: _____

Topic sentence

(key point): _____

Facts, figures, graphics _____

(list, if appropriate): _____

Transition: _____

Paragraph 3

Heading: _____

Topic sentence

(key point): _____

Facts, figures, graphics _____

(list, if appropriate): _____

Transition: _____

Concluding Paragraph

Heading: _____

Summary: _____

_____

_____

Action items _____

(priority, what, _____

who, deadlines): _____

PROOF POINT!

Directions: Compare the following versions of a goodwill letter sent to thank clients for selecting a real estate firm to market their property. Explain which version of the letter best addresses the needs of the reader and is easiest to read. Circle specific examples of letter content that prove your points. Which version contains more awkward, clumsy content?

You're in Good Hands
with
GLOBAL REALTY

May 20, 200-

Dear Mr. Jackson:

As broker of GLOBAL REALTY, I would like to thank you for choosing this office to market your property. We will apply to your property the proven market techniques that have already given us many happy, satisfied clients.

I am very proud to announce that this year marks our twentieth anniversary of servicing the Treasure Valley's real estate needs. Our office specializes in commerical/business investments, farm and ranch sales, residential resale, and new construction. We have 80 agents in our office, and we publish our own advertising magazine monthly. When you chose GLOBAL REALTY, you enlisted the services of over 100,000 Realtors with the "Power to Move" real estate.

As we join with you in this team effort to find a buyer for your property, please feel free to contact me at any time. If you have a question or want a briefing on the progress of the marketing procedures on your property, call me at 208-555-0100.

Sincerely,

Lucinda Pratt
Broker

Global Realty Letter Version 1

PROOF POINT! (continued)

You're in Good Hands
with
GLOBAL REALTY

May 20, 200-

Dear Mr. Jackson:

<u>Thank you</u> for selecting GLOBAL REALTY to market your home. Our goal is to get the best price for your property in the shortest possible time. <u>You can depend on us</u> **for many reasons:**

- <u>You</u> are working with the largest and most successful real estate company in the world. Our worldwide network increases the sales market for your property by over 50 percent compared to those agencies limited to local marketing.

- **In addition,** <u>your</u> property will be marketed by the largest and most productive local real estate agency, with 100 agents representing you.

- Our advertising is the most widespread in the industry. **Consequently,** we reach a broader base of potential buyers for your property than any other real estate organization.

- <u>You</u> have **also** selected the most reputable local firm. Our 20 years of successful and respected service in the Treasure Valley give you unmatched professional visibility and sales advantage.

<u>You</u> can count on us to market your property aggressively and professionally with the goal of securing the best sale as quickly as possible. Please contact me personally to discuss any questions you may have concerning the marketing of your property. My number is 208-555-0100.

Sincerely,

Lucinda Pratt
Broker

Global Realty Letter Version 2

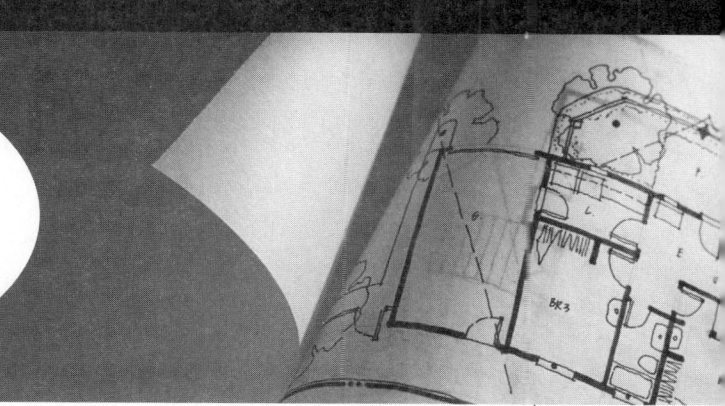

Sound Blueprints

Objectives	After completing Chapter 8, you will be able to: • Plan and organize your message. • Choose the best organizational pattern. • Write effective introductions and closings. • Use the direct pattern for results-oriented messages. • Develop persuasive messages logically. • Use the indirect pattern for bad news.

PLANNING AND ORGANIZATION

You'll benefit greatly from organizing your ideas before you start to write. The writing task will be much simpler, your message will be more effective, and your planning will reduce the need for revisions.

This chapter will guide you in planning and organizing your message to best achieve your writing objective—influencing your reader to respond or take the action you want.

Prepare to Speed Process and Increase Quality

In the fast-paced business world, people tend to rush to get to the core of a task. Eagerness to "get to the writing" can jeopardize quality as the writer skimps on the planning and organizing phase. Just as a well-built foundation is essential for a home, planning and organizing create a strong foundation for writing. This step also speeds the writing process; it eliminates the need for rework to correct organizational problems midstream.

Set up an idea file for major projects. To write a message requiring detailed research and writing (such as a report, project management outline, or proposal), set up an idea file on the topic. Put information you gather on the topic in this file. If your writing project is extensive, you may need to prepare several files for related subtopics.

Gather data, resource materials, and supplies. Assemble all of the reference materials you need and review them carefully before you begin writing. This step helps you avoid the frustration and inefficiency of stopping to find resources just when your thoughts start flowing. Gather the following:

- Previous correspondence related to the subject

- Files and other documents related to the subject

- Names and addresses of your readers

- Other materials (pamphlets, product or service information, catalogs, enclosures you intend to send, etc.)

Review Resources

Review your resource materials (previous correspondence, file documents, etc.) to familiarize yourself with the details of the subject. Highlight or underline important items; and jot down those ideas on a notepad, or key them on your computer. This preparation will focus your ideas for the next step, clustering.

Use Clustering to Brainstorm Main Ideas

Review the guidelines presented in Chapter 1 for using the clustering method to brainstorm and generate your initial ideas. Study your key ideas; add to them, if necessary; and arrange them in logical order for effective development of your message.

Clarify Your Purpose

Good writing is well focused and requires developing a clear answer to the primary question "What is my purpose?" Ask yourself whether your purpose is to:

- Request information or to provide information.

- Sell an idea or a product.

- Persuade the reader to take action or make a response.

- Collect payment.

- Apologize for a problem.

- Congratulate the reader.

Use "The Writer's Planning Guide"

The "Writer's Planning Guide," which follows, will help you plan and organize your ideas. Once you've responded to all of the questions, review your answers to spot areas of weakness. Make note of additional information you need to answer each question adequately. Then follow up by getting the information. This follow-up separates good writers from mediocre writers; it's essential for developing clear, complete messages.

By answering each question in the "Writer's Planning Guide" before you begin writing, you create a clear direction for your message. In addition, you will avoid omitting pertinent information, your message will be more persuasive, and you will better succeed in getting the results you want.

 TIP *You can customize your own writer's planning guide by including those questions that are most relevant to your typical writing projects.*

WRITER'S PLANNING GUIDE

1. **WHY AM I WRITING?** What is my purpose? Is it to inform, request, or persuade? Do I have another purpose? (Refer to your cluster outline.)

2. **WHAT IS THE MAIN MESSAGE?** What is the main idea I want to communicate? (This is the focus statement from the cluster outline.)

3. **WHAT ACTION IS REQUESTED?**
   - What do I want my reader to do?
   - What is the deadline?

4. **WHO IS THE READER?**
   - How can I write to meet the needs of the reader—keeping in mind personality type, educational level, etc.?
   - Which writing style (formal or less formal) and tone (amiable, formal, or firm) are appropriate? Why?

5. **WHAT IS THE *WIFM?*** What's in it for the reader? (Remember to present benefits first.)

6. **IS MY MESSAGE CREDIBILE?**
   - What facts will convince my reader, and how much does the reader need to know?
   - What are the most credible sources I can cite?
   - What other information is needed to support the purpose? Where can I get the information?

7. **WHICH ORGANIZATIONAL PATTERN WILL BE BEST?** Is it chronological, order-of-importance, etc.? (This topic is discussed in the following section.)

8. **HOW CAN I ESTABLISH RAPPORT?** What courteous and/or personal words can I use to establish or enhance rapport?

9. **IS IT COMPLETE?** Have I appropriately answered the questions *who, what, why, where, when, how,* and *how much?*

10. **WHICH ORGANIZATIONAL REQUIREMENTS APPLY?** Have I followed the document development and formatting requirements of my organization?

ORGANIZATIONAL PATTERNS

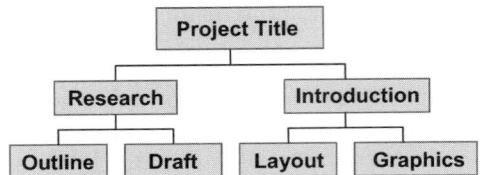

Good writing is coherent—the ideas are presented in the most logical order and pattern. Several methods of organization are possible. The most appropriate choice depends on your purpose and the type of information you are communicating. To strengthen all of your written communications, consider which pattern will be most effective for each message. The following patterns are appropriate for a number of business documents.

Order-of-Importance Pattern

Use this pattern to emphasize the most significant point first, followed by items presented in descending order of importance. The following example highlights the most salable features of a home.

- All new shake roof
- New kitchen appliances
- Newly painted interior

Chronological Pattern

Use this pattern to (a) describe a natural time sequence of events; (b) describe a process; or (c) give instructions, including safety instructions. Chronological order leads the reader through historical development of a topic, guides the reader through required steps, or indicates the most efficient responses or actions.

Space Pattern

This pattern is useful for expressing spatial or physical relationships, such as those involved in giving directions or describing a floor plan. The content is enhanced with an illustration or an appropriate graphic.

- Place Part A at a right angle to Part B. Fasten together with. . . .
- Come to the administration building, which is at the far end of our parking lot. Enter the front door, and take the elevator to the sixth floor. Turn right, and go down the hall to the third office on the left.

General-to-Specific Pattern

Appropriate for lengthy or technical documents, this pattern communicates well to several levels of readers. It provides a quick overview of the key points at the beginning of the document for readers who are responsible for being informed only of the general concepts. The specific details follow for those readers who are responsible for more technical assessment or use of the material.

Problem/Cause/Solution Pattern

Use this pattern to explain the process of solving a problem. Define the problem, explain the methods used to solve it, describe results and effectiveness, and present your conclusions and recommendations.

Direct Pattern

This pattern presents the main idea or conclusion first, followed by the data necessary to support the idea or conclusion. Use this format when you expect a neutral or favorable reader reaction. This is the most common pattern for business e-mail, letters, and memos.

Indirect Pattern

This pattern presents the facts, supporting data, and/or reasons first and leads the reader to a logical conclusion. Use this pattern if you think the reader will disagree with or have an unfavorable reaction to the message. Because the indirect pattern focuses attention on the supportive facts and reasons, this pattern is more persuasive than the direct style.

ACTIVITY 8.1

Directions: On the blank line next to each situation listed below, write the letter of the most effective organizational pattern.

O = Order-of-Importance
C = Chronological
S = Space
G = General-to-Specific
P = Problem/Cause/Solution
D = Direct
I = Indirect

1. _____ Explaining a production error and how it has been solved by your unit

2. _____ Writing instructions for a new procedure for your area

3. _____ Describing for your boss the quarterly accomplishments of your department or unit

ACTIVITY 8.1 continued

4. _____ Presenting a proposal to a management committee that has traditionally held a negative view of the idea

5. _____ Describing an electrical system for a new building or describing how to assemble a piece of equipment

6. _____ Writing a proposal or recommendation that contains a significant amount of technical detail

EFFECTIVE INTRODUCTIONS AND CLOSINGS

First and last impressions are vital. In written communications, the biggest impact is made at the beginning of the message. The closing is the part of the message that makes the next biggest impact on the reader. This section of the chapter provides guidelines for writing strong introductions and closings that keep people reading and that encourage positive responses and reactions.

Follow Guidelines for Effective Introductions

The introduction sets the tone and establishes your credibility; it also may determine whether your reader decides to finish reading the message. Because the success or failure of your entire message may rest on your introduction, give this part of your message focused attention. The following guidelines will help you write introductions that are persuasive and that make a positive impression.

Get to the point. Readers want to know what the purpose of the message is. In most cases, you should state the main idea in your first paragraph. The exception is a bad news message, which requires a buffer introduction to set a courteous tone. Compare the following two examples. Which message would you rather receive?

- In reply to your letter of May 18, we reviewed all of our records thoroughly to determine if we received your final payment. After two weeks, we finally found the verification we needed. Please note that your final payment has been recorded.

- Yes, we received your final payment, and your loan is paid in full.

Avoid a cliché introduction. Beginning messages with clichés is a poor way to establish credibility.

Poor: This is in reply to your letter of. . . .

Better: The products you ordered on March 8 were shipped today.

If the message is positive, say so immediately. Review the following examples of positive introductions:

- Yes, we can reserve the conference room for you on October 20.

- Thank you for. . . .
- You'll be happy to know. . . .

Remember the *WIFM*. If you are writing to convince your reader, put the benefits up front—highlight them in the introduction. Try to emphasize in your first sentence the idea that will most interest or benefit your reader.

- Your message will reach over 50,000 listeners when you advertise with our radio station.

Consider starting with a question. When writing a sales or proposal letter, consider starting with one or more questions that relate to your purpose. Questions encourage readers to respond mentally, thereby increasing their involvement.

- Winter is fast approaching. Have you winterized your sprinkling system yet?

Whenever possible, start with the *you emphasis*. Don't begin with the *I/we emphasis*.

Poor: We encourage you to take advantage of our special half-off price on all items in stock.

Better: You can save a full 50 percent on. . . .

Don't present bad news up front. However, don't bury the bad news, but convey it thoughtfully.

Poor: We cannot use your manuscript at this time. It is being returned with this letter.

Better: Thank you for submitting the manuscript of your article on desktop publishing innovations. Our manuscript panel evaluated your article carefully, and the members concurred that we cannot justify another article on the subject after last month's extensive coverage of related desktop publishing issues.

Poor: We can't approve an extension on your payment date.

Better: Although we appreciate your concerns, you have been granted the maximum number of extensions. We are unable to meet your request.

Follow Guidelines for Effective Closings

Keep in mind that readers remember best what they read first and last. This fact is fundamental to successful writing and can work to your advantage. Use the closing to reemphasize your purpose and to stimulate your reader to carry out the action you're seeking.

Help your reader understand. Summarize or emphasize your main points. This is especially important for complex messages.

Motivate your reader to act. Request a reply or action, specify a date, and explain the need for the requested action or reply. This encourages a timely response. The term *as soon as possible* is too vague.

  Poor: Send your quarterly budget proposal directly to me so we can review it.

  Better: Please send your quarterly budget proposal directly to me by May 4 so we can review it by phone and allow time for any necessary corrections.

End with an upbeat tone that implies a positive reaction. Avoid conveying a lack of confidence or any hint of expected negative reaction.

  Poor: *I hope* you will find that this proposal meets your needs.

  Better: This proposal has been designed to meet all of the customized conditions you specified.

  Poor: *If you are interested* in learning more about this innovative mutual investment plan, call Tom Clark at 555-0128.

  Better: To learn more about this innovative. . . .

Don't use a cliché ending. Clichés project an outdated image.

  Poor: If I may be of further service, do not hesitate to call.

  Better: Please call if you need more information.

Express instructions positively, and include deadlines to motivate action. Strengthen the final impression you leave by addressing the needs of the reader once more.

  Poor: Please send your reply no later than July 30.

  Better: We can include your company name in the fall business directory if you return your application by July 30.

DIRECT PATTERN FOR RESULTS-ORIENTED MESSAGES

Good writers appeal to the needs of the receiver(s). Good writers also get to the point, stay on the topic, and emphasize required or requested action. The **direct pattern,** explained below, is the most efficient and effective style for writing standard business documents. However, writing bad news messages requires a more subtle approach, which is explained later in the chapter.

Typically, readers have three primary questions as they begin to read a business message:

1. *WIFM:* What's in it for me (positive, negative, neutral)?

2. Do I have to take any action?

3. What is the priority, and what is the deadline?

The direct pattern addresses those three issues quickly, emphasizes reader benefits, uses formatting techniques to clarify details, and includes an effective subject line.

STEP 1 — Broadcast purpose, deadline, and benefits at the beginning.

To help your reader begin to comprehend your message quickly, make your purpose clear from the beginning.

  • **In the subject line:** Headline purpose and deadline in a clear, abbreviated statement.

- **In the first paragraph:** Write your complete purpose or *focus statement.*
- **In the first paragraph:** Emphasize any benefits (*WIFM*) to the reader and/or organization.

STEP 2 — Provide details.

In the body of your message, focus on the details.

- Include information: facts, figures, and graphic data.
- Add persuasive and supportive statements.

 TIP   *Use headings and lists to emphasize and clarify details.*

STEP 3 — Use an effective closing.

Create a results-oriented ending that calls for action or summarizes important points.

- Reemphasize key points, the requested action(s), and any deadline.
- Build rapport.
- Focus on the reader's needs.

Write a Specific, Not General, Subject Line

Write a specific subject line that clearly identifies the purpose of the document, and include a deadline when appropriate. When you use a subject line that is too general, the reader is unable to grasp the central message. A specific subject line also helps the reader transition to the body of the message and comprehend it quickly.

Compare each pair of subject lines below. Notice that the second example in each pair is more specific and, therefore, more useful to the reader for grasping the purpose of the message quickly.

- Forwarding Invoice #682
  Process Invoice #682 for Routers by May 4
- Information Regarding Laptop Computers
  Increase Field Staff Efficiency with Laptop Computers

 TIP   *To write an action-oriented subject line:*

- Include a term that clearly represents the main topic.
- If appropriate, include a verb that indicates required or desired action.

ACTIVITY 8.2

Directions: Write a subject line for a message you need to send in the near future. Make the subject line as specific as possible.

_____

_____

ACTIVITY 8.3

Directions: Mark revisions to the memo below to apply the direct pattern techniques. Answer the following questions to help you identify the weaknesses in this memo and to mark your corrections to it.

1. What is the purpose of the memo?

2. Is the subject line specific or general in content?

3. In what part of the memo does the purpose appear? Are benefits clearly emphasized in the first paragraph? Explain.

4. Where are the details provided? Are these details formatted as clearly as possible?

5. Is the closing effective? Explain.

 **Tennis Racquets Unlimited**

TO: Marketing Supervisors

FROM: Helen Soga, Manager

DATE: July 12, 200-

SUBJECT: ADVERTISING SLOGAN

Attached is the slogan selection form that lists the three choices submitted by our advertising committee. Also attached are samples of our ad layout. Each sample incorporates one of the three slogans.

Use this form to select the slogan for our new Xenith model racquet. We want to begin the advertising campaign for this model on time so we can increase Christmas sales.

To complete the slogan selection form, please do the following: Compare each sample ad layout, mark the box next to the slogan you prefer, and write a brief explanation at the bottom explaining why the slogan you chose is most effective.

Please return your completed selection form to me as soon as possible so we can meet our ad preparation deadline.

Compare the revision below to the draft of the sample memo on the preceding page. Notice how applying the direct pattern to the draft conveys the message more clearly and persuasively and how the memo more effectively calls for action. The writer enhances the clarity of this message by using a heading and a list. Both of these techniques make information stand out visually. In addition, in giving instructions, the writer has used the most effective mode possible—the command. Use these same writing strategies to your advantage.

 **Tennis Racquets Unlimited**

TO: Marketing Supervisors

FROM: Helen Soga, Manager

DATE: July 12, 200-

SUBJECT: SELECT SLOGAN FOR XENITH BY JULY 17

We need your help in selecting the slogan for our new Xenith model racquet. Please indicate your choice on the attached selection form. If we meet our target date of August 1 to begin our advertising campaign, we will increase Christmas sales. As a result, you may receive increased bonuses. Procedures for selecting the slogan are outlined in this memo.

Attached is the slogan selection form that lists the three slogan choices submitted by our advertising committee. Also attached are samples of the ad layout. Each sample incorporates one of the three slogans.

Procedures for Completing Slogan Selection Form

Follow these procedures to complete the slogan selection form:

1. Compare each sample ad layout.

2. On the slogan selection form, mark the box next to the slogan you prefer.

3. Write a brief explanation at the bottom of the selection form explaining why the slogan you chose is most effective.

Please return your completed selection form to me by July 17 so we can meet our ad preparation deadline.

Attachment

PERSUASIVE MESSAGES

Effectively persuading a reader to accept your conclusions or arguments requires credible development of your message. Techniques for achieving this goal are outlined in this section.

Persuasive writing requires applying critical-thinking skills—providing reasons supporting a stated conclusion or claim in an effort to convince the reader to arrive at the same conclusion.

Provide a Sound Argument

When writing to convince your reader of a debatable conclusion, you need to provide a sound argument. An argument contains three elements:

- A stated *main issue*

- One or more stated *reasons* (called *premises* in logic) for the issue

- One or more stated *conclusions*

In other words, to write persuasively, you need to develop sound arguments supported by valid data or facts that prove the reasons for your conclusions.

Use a Direct, Persuasive Pattern

To write a persuasive message using the direct pattern, follow these three steps:

1. **Introduction:** State your main idea, purpose, or proposal. This section might also include background on the issue and a brief statement explaining how your idea provides a solution.

2. **Body of Message:**

   a. State additional points required to support your main idea.

   b. Provide observable and verifiable evidence or data that prove your main points, and document the source of the data.

3. **Closing:** State conclusions or recommendations and state required actions based on the evidence or data presented. Emphasize the benefits or outcomes of your proposal.

 TIP *To persuade readers who oppose your idea, use the indirect pattern:*

- Do not lead with the main purpose.

- Develop a skillful argument.

- Lead the reader to your conclusion.

INDIRECT PATTERN FOR BAD NEWS

The indirect pattern is appropriate for delivering bad news or refusal messages as well as messages requiring skillful persuasion (particularly directed at readers who may not initially support your objective). In this format, you don't lead with the direct topic; you ease into it and develop it persuasively.

Opening Use a courteous buffer opening, and maintain the dignity of the receiver. Soften the impact, and encourage a receptive tone. Put yourself in the reader's shoes. One of these techniques may be appropriate:

- Thank the reader for the inquiry, application, payment, suggestion, etc.
- Emphasize any positive aspect of the situation.

Reasons and Explanation Present the bad news or refusal.

- Emphasize the careful consideration and review your organization has given to the situation.
- Give the reason for the bad news or refusal.

Decision Make it clear.

- Avoid canned explanations or accusations such as: "It's against company policy," "Please understand," "You claim," or "You state."
- Do not express the decision in a one-sentence paragraph.
- If necessary, make a firm, yet friendly request for action by a specified date.

Counter-Proposal Offer an alternative or assistance if appropriate.

Close Make it positive.

- Use a goodwill or action closing if offering a counterproposal.
- Avoid using negative terms.

 TIP *Keep the following reminders in mind when writing bad-news messages:*

- ✓ **Maintain a positive tone**, but don't make it overly optimistic.
- ✓ **Send a personally addressed and formatted letter.** Do not use a blatantly impersonal form letter or a form with items checked.
- ✓ **Avoid negative words** such as *refuse, turn down, reject, disappoint, failure, defective, inferior, trouble, cannot,* and *no.*
- ✓ **Focus on maintaining the reader's esteem** with tact and courtesy. Visualize writing the message to your best friend and choosing words carefully.
- ✓ **Avoid the three Ds.** Do not use a tone that is demanding, demoralizing, or demeaning.

Notice how the indirect pattern is used in this bad-news letter to courteously convey negative news.

February 12, 200-

Mr. Frank Sheehan
4266 Imperial Way
Austin, TX 78710

Dear Mr. Sheehan:

Buffer	Thank you for your proposal to provide customer service training for Weston Company customer service representatives. We appreciate your promptness in submitting the proposal for review by our professional development committee.
Reasons and explanation	Eight well-qualified training organizations submitted bids, and they were exceptionally competitive. Our customer service needs are not common, and we require uniquely tailored training materials. While your proposal is professional and thorough, it is not directly customized for our industry. For this reason, we have selected a proposal that is designed
Decision	specifically for our distinctive industry needs.
Goodwill and future rapport	We would be pleased to consider future proposals from your organization. I would be happy to meet with you to discuss other areas of training you have developed that may be appropriate for our company.
Close	I look forward to hearing from you soon.

Sincerely,

Corina Lang
Director
Human Resources and Development

PROOF POINT!

Directions: Match the power tools listed below with the sentences in the paragraph following the list. On the line next to each of the listed power tools, write the number of the sentence that would be improved by using that power tool.

Sentence Number	Power Tools
_____	Include a *WIFM* (or benefit) where appropriate.
_____	Eliminate dummy subjects.
_____	Use lists to clarify details.
_____	Use deadlines to motivate action.
_____	Use active and passive voice effectively.

(1) A meeting of our finance committee will be held to develop the annual budget. (2) There are four items we will consider during this meeting: equipment, computer software training, travel, and remodeling expenses. (3) To ensure adequate planning, please send me your suggestions as soon as possible regarding each of these budget items.

Formatting and Fine-Tuning Tools

Objectives

After completing Chapter 9, you will be able to:

- Use the appropriate document: e-mail, memo, or letter.
- Format documents correctly.
- Compose and format results-oriented e-mail messages.
- Eliminate outdated terms.
- Avoid redundancies.
- Avoid long-winded and abstract terms.
- Use specific, measurable terms.
- Eliminate qualifiers.

E-MAIL, MEMO, OR LETTER

Base your choice of document format on the type of message you are writing and the purpose of the message. This section of Chapter 9 discusses memos, letters, and e-mail messages. In addition, it provides expanded guidelines for writing and formatting efficient and results-oriented e-mail messages.

E-mail

E-mail is used to communicate day-to-day information quickly and efficiently. It is somewhat less formal than a memo. (More detailed information regarding e-mail messages is presented later in this chapter.) However, some internal business situations require the more formal memo format. For example, a memo is preferred for notifying employees of important policy changes, but an e-mail message is sufficient to remind committee members of an upcoming meeting.

Memo

An interoffice memorandum, or memo, is the appropriate choice for sending a brief written message *inside* a business organization. The primary purpose of a memo is to communicate concisely and clearly—to take care of business quickly and efficiently. The memo is more formal in structure and content than an e-mail message and is typically less formal than a letter. A memo is usually written in an action-oriented, informal style.

Letter

A letter is the best document format for writing formal business messages to people outside the organization. Letters create the all-important first impression of the organization through the format and content. This document is appropriate for more lengthy content than what is typically conveyed in a memo or an e-mail message. Letters are also the most appropriate choice for content that may be important for future reference or documentation, such as legal information.

Tips for Results-Oriented Documents

Follow the guidelines below to write letters, memos, and e-mail messages that produce the results you want:

1. Tell your reader the main idea in the subject line (except when writing a bad-news message). Be specific enough that your reader can grasp the main idea.

2. Keep your messages as short as possible.

3. Use short, direct sentences and paragraphs.

4. Limit your messages to one primary topic.

5. Highlight key points:

    • Use numbered, lettered, or bulleted lists to highlight key points.

    • Use headings to summarize paragraphs.

    • Use font enhancements where appropriate (bold, italics, and underline).

6. Clearly define responsibility for action, indicating who is responsible for what and by what date.

DOCUMENT FORMATS

To project professionalism, business documents need to be formatted correctly following expected business standards. This section of Chapter 9 presents document models for your reference in formatting business letters, memos, and e-mail messages.

Letterhead	**·AXION·**
	2200 Alta Street • Tampa, FL 33607-2123 • axion@clausson.net
Date	January 15, 200-- DS
Addressee notation	**CONFIDENTIAL** QS
Attention line **Inside address** **when individual** **name is unknown**	Attention Accounting Department Casper Unlimited 1655 Raven Avenue Raleigh, NC 27612-6904 DS
Salutation when **name is unknown**	Ladies and Gentlemen: DS
Subject line	PROSPECTIVE PAYMENT PLAN DS
Body	**** ***** ***** *** ******* ** ** ******** *** **** **** **** **** **** *** ***** **** ***. * **** * **** ***** *** ******* ** * ***** *** *** *** **** **** **** **** * *** *** ***** **** ************************************.
Complimentary close	Sincerely, QS
Writer **Writer's title**	Michelle Johnson Senior Vice President DS
Reference initials	tds DS
Enclosure notation	Enclosure (or Enclosures 2) DS
Copy notation	c Tre'jon Mack DS
Postscript	**** **** **** **** ***** ** * ***************.

Business Letter Components (Every line begins at left margin, and standard punctuation is used.)

DOCUMENT FORMATS

Langworth Associates

280 Ralston Drive
Cincinnati, Ohio 45227-0076 (513) 555-0117

Date	June 16, 200-
	QS
Inside address	Ms. Anita Cepeda
	2008 Lyon Way
	Yuma, AZ 85367-5450
	DS
Salutation	Dear Ms. Cepeda:
	DS
Subject line	SEEKING SYSTEMS ANALYST
	DS

Body ****** **** **** **** **** ** *** * **** *** *** ** *** **** *** ** * **** ***
****** **** **** **** **** ** *** * **** *** *** ** *** **** *** ** * **** ***
****** **** **** **** **** ** *** * **** *** *** ** *** **** ****. **DS**

****** **** **** **** **** ** *** * **** *** *** ** *** **** *** ** * **** ***
****** **** **** **** **** ** *** * **** *** *** ** *** **** *** ** * **** ***
****** **** **** **** **** ** *** * **** *** *** ** *** **** ****. **DS**

Complimentary close	Sincerely,
	QS
Writer	Robert Horton
Writer's title	Human Relations Manager
	DS
Enclosure notation	Enclosure

Letter in Block Format (standard punctuation)

DOCUMENT FORMATS

Shelton Enterprises

642 Ralley Street

Palatine, Illinois 60074-1975 (847) 555-0193

Date	January 15, 200-
Inside address	Mr. Harold Tanabe Javray Inc. 1247 Madison Road Phoenixville, PA 19460
Salutation	Dear Mr. Tanabe:
Subject line	ANNUAL SERVICE PROPOSAL
Body	***** ***** ***** ***** ***** ***** ********* ****** ***** ***** ***** ***** ***** ***** ********* ******.
Divided paragraph (at least two lines on first page)	***** *** ** * **** ***** *** * ***** **** ******* ** ******* **** ***** ***** **** *** *** ***** *******. **** ***** **** ***** ***** ***** ***** ****** ***** ********* * **** *** ***. ***** ********* *****.

Page 1 of Two-Page Business Letter

Second-page heading	Mr. Harold Tanabe Page 2 January 15, 200-
Continued paragraph (at least a full line on second page)	***** ***** ***** ***** ***** ***** ***** ***** ****** ***** **. ***** ***** ***** ***** ***** ***** ***** ***** ****** ******* **** ***** ***** **** *** *** ***** **** ****.
Complimentary close	Sincerely,
Writer **Writer's title**	Devonna Washington, Director Medical Records

Page 2 of Two-Page Business Letter

DOCUMENT FORMATS

TO: Corey Langley

FROM: Nan Okasaki

DATE: May 18, 200-

SUBJECT: TECHNICAL WRITING WORKSHOP, JULY 12 AND 14

Please prepare a formal training contract including the following information: The trainer is Victor G. Mena. His address is 140 Sky Way, Savannah, Georgia 31401-9229; telephone: (912) 555-0166.

One workshop of Technical Writing training, consisting of 12 hours total, is to be scheduled from 9 a.m. to noon and from 1 p.m. to 4 p.m. on Tuesday, July 12, and Thursday, July 14. The fee for each participant is $150. The target class size is 15. Victor will provide the instructional workbook for each participant, and Weston Associates will provide the classroom and equipment.

Please arrange to have the following equipment available for Victor on the days the training is scheduled: an LCD projector, a projector screen, and a podium.

Memo 1: No Highlighting Techniques Used (details are buried; no action date is specified)

DOCUMENT FORMATS

TO: Corey Langley

FROM: Brenda Swenson

DATE: May 18, 200-

SUBJECT: TECHNICAL WRITING WORKSHOP, JULY 12 AND 14

Please prepare a formal training contract including the following information:

Trainer Information

    Victor G. Mena; 140 Sky Way, Savannah, Georgia 31401-9229;
(912) 555-0166

Course Title, Number of Participants, Instructional Materials, Fee

Title:	Technical Writing Workshop
Participants:	Target class size of 15
Materials:	Instructional workbooks (provided by Victor Mena)
Fee:	$150 per participant

Schedule: One 12-hour course of Technical Writing, scheduled as follows:

Dates:	Tuesday, July 12, and Thursday, July 14
Times:	9 a.m. to noon and 1 p.m. to 4 p.m. daily

Equipment Needs: Make arrangements to have the following equipment available each day:

- An LCD projector
- A projection screen
- A podium

Please send me a copy of the proposal no later than May 25.

Memo 2: Highlighting Techniques Used (details stand out; action date is specified)

RESULTS-ORIENTED E-MAIL MESSAGES

E-mail provides many benefits in business communication. For example, people reduce project development time significantly by using e-mail to communicate and transmit information quickly. By managing e-mail efficiently and applying the techniques from *Power Tools for Business Writing*, you can attract reader attention and increase your productivity.

Tools for Writing Powerful E-mail Messages

Follow these specific guidelines to write clear, action-oriented e-mail messages that have a positive reader impact.

1. **Meet the needs of the recipients.** Consider the needs of your audience, and be aware of professional expectations. Appeal to busy recipients by keeping messages short and by limiting yourself to one subject per message, but include all information the recipient needs to take appropriate action and to reach you. Try to limit the entire message to one screen.

   a. In the To line, list only those recipients who must take action. Sending messages to anyone who doesn't need them is inefficient.

   b. In the Cc line, list those recipients who need to know but aren't assigned action items.

2. **Write an action-oriented subject line.** A well-written subject line is essential. Recipients may read or ignore an e-mail message based on the subject.

   Summarize the topic in as few words as possible. Follow with a verb that expresses the action requested. Consider the audience (superior, peer, subordinate) when determining the appropriate wording. Use consistent key words in related subject lines to help readers locate messages by topic when they sort their in-boxes by subject.

   - Permit Application: Please Read by May 2

   - Permit Application: Action Items Due May 7

   - Permit Application: Need Data by May 12

3. **Write a clear introduction.** Follow the guidelines below to write an effective introduction:

   a. **Include an initial heading.** When appropriate, write a heading to identify the primary topic.

   b. **Describe the purpose.** Add detail not covered in the subject line, provide a sense of perspective, and define the level of urgency.

   c. **Describe the action required.** If appropriate, briefly describe the action (for example, making a decision, providing technical data, and answering a question).

4. **Develop the body.** Use headings and lists to clarify details and to outline required action items.

   a. **Label sections with headings.** Include boldfaced headings in the body to label key topics and desired actions, expanding on key introductory topics. In some cases, using all capital letters in headings is helpful.

b. **Write lists when possible.**

- Use a numbered list to indicate the priority or the required order of actions. Use numbers for lists of more than three items to help readers avoid skipping items as they read and to help them reference individual items quickly. Numbers provide a clearer chronological sequence than bullets.

- Use bulleted lists for one to three items when priority is not an issue.

c. **Include action items.** Action items should clearly state the task, the person or group responsible, and the deadline.

5. **Write a conclusion.** Address the following items in the conclusion:

a. **Introduce the conclusion with a heading to identify the section, if appropriate.**

b. **Briefly summarize the message; and emphasize the key points, where appropriate.**

c. **Include any recommendations you have.**

- If you don't have a recommendation, ask for feedback and direction, when appropriate.

- If you didn't include them earlier, list action items with names of people responsible for them and the deadlines.

6. **Use the automatic signature feature of your e-mail software.** Include your e-mail address, phone number(s), pager number, and other contact information.

7. **Apply these "professional e-mail power tools."** The following techniques and practices are also important for developing clear, professional e-mail messages:

- **Use an effective font.** Use a 12-point Verdana or Georgia font. These fonts were specifically designed for viewing on computer monitors. Smaller fonts can be difficult to read and may elicit a negative response because the message looks too busy. Use bold to emphasize headings and key points, but don't overdo it.

- **Generally use the standard mix of uppercase and lowercase letters.** Except in occasional headings, do not use all capital letters. Doing so is like SHOUTING and is hard to read. Readers cannot distinguish proper nouns in text that is all one case. Do not use all lowercase letters. These are hard to read, and they are grammatically incorrect. Terms that should be capitalized are not, and the pronoun *I* becomes *i*.

- **Keep the tone of your messages positive.** Avoid angry outbursts (flaming).

- **Minimize the number of e-mail messages.** Instead, call or meet face-to-face when appropriate. However, writing is preferred over telephoning for those who speak English as a second language. Writing is easier to comprehend because the reader can see and review the content, which is not possible in a telephone conversation.

- **Avoid sending e-mail messages explaining every detail of progress.** Allow some time for resolution of issues before communicating.

- **Don't assume privacy.** E-mail is a tool provided by employers, and employers have the right to view all e-mail messages.

- **Be professional.** Don't subject your reader to sloppy content. As with hard-copy documents, your professional reputation is reflected in your e-mail messages:
  - Plan and organize the message.
  - Prepare a draft; proofread and revise it.
  - Avoid emoticons.
  - Be careful using humor.
  - Avoid sarcasm.
- **Limit personal messages.** If personal messages are permitted in your organization, keep them to a minimum.

Tips for Managing E-mail Efficiently

In addition to writing action-oriented e-mail messages, managing e-mail is essential to achieving productivity. The following tips will help you achieve this objective.

- Proofread, check grammar and spelling, and correct errors before sending. Use the automatic grammar/spelling checker, but do not trust it. Spelling checkers and grammar checkers are not infallible; proofread every word. Ask another person to read critical e-mail messages before you send them.
- Avoid long e-mail strings. Avoid forwarding long e-mail message strings unless absolutely necessary. If you do forward a string of e-mail messages, summarize the string at the beginning of the message and revise the recipient list as appropriate.
- Keep e-mail messages organized in topical folders for quick access. For example, e-mail can be efficiently organized in folders by topic, by date due, by name of sender, and by project.
- Consider attachments. Find out if your recipient is allowed to receive attachments—don't assume. To avoid forgetting your attachment, attach the document first; then write your message.
- Store sent messages. Keep sent messages until action is completed or for future access in case you need to resend.
- Check the address before you click Send.

Responses to E-mail Messages

Follow these guidelines when replying to e-mail messages:

1. Answer promptly. If you can't respond completely, reply indicating when you can.

2. Read the entire message first. Some writers bury important information.

3. Answer all questions completely.

4. Comment directly in the sender's message. Use a different font type or color to comment or respond to content or questions in the body of the sender's e-mail. This helps senders match your response to their message.

E-mail Format

The e-mail techniques presented in this chapter are incorporated in the following model. This is the recommended format for writing results-oriented and reader-friendly e-mail.

To:	nstclair
From:	msmith
Cc:	jdorland; toliver; ecamarillo
Subject:	CRITICAL NEW BUSINESS: ANSWER QUESTIONS–ARRANGE MEETING
Date:	March 31, 200-

Message:

BUSINESS OPPORTUNITY: NEED YOUR HELP ON TWO ACTIONS

Subject line: Main topic and action required

Chips-On-A-Stick (COAS) is developing a design for a high-volume PC chipset that could result in a major business opportunity for us. I'm planning the design with them and need your help with the following:

Introduction expands main topic and action required

1. **Please provide technical information:** COAS engineers need immediate information about the following items. Please send the information to Tevi Lawson at this address: tlawson@coas.com.

   • Critical product specifications

   • Summary of advantages of our chips

Numbered list with boldfaced headers emphasizes key actions required

2. **Arrange a meeting.** The lead chipset designer for COAS will be in the United States April 10-15. Please arrange a meeting with our lead engineers at our main site. Let me know by 1 p.m. tomorrow which day and time will work.

Top Priority

This project is critical, and your quick response to this request to send product information and arrange a meeting is important to our success.

Conclusion summarizes actions

Nadine St. Clair
Design Engineer, Product Development
Fast Chips, Inc.

E-mail:	ns@fci.com
Phone:	206-555-0182
Address:	1205 Koch Lane
	Seattle, WA 98116

Automatic signature provides complete contact information: name, title, company, e-mail address, phone number, mailing address

E-Mail Message

OUTDATED TERMS

Worn-out clichés do little to promote a progressive, up-to-date image for you or your organization. They diminish the credibility and force of your message. These expressions also create an insincere and impersonal tone, implying that you have given little thought or energy to developing the communication. Strengthen your writing by eliminating any cliche's during your final proofreading and editing phase.

Outdated Expression	**Correction**
1. For your information	Omit the phrase. Obviously, you are writing for the reader's information.
2. Please advise me	Don't use *advise* to mean "tell" or "inform."
3. As per	*As* or *according to*
4. This is to inform (advise) you	Omit the phrase. It is unnecessary.
5. Wish to say	If you have something to say, say it!
6. Pursuant to your request; in accordance with your request	*As you requested* sounds more natural.
7. For the balance of the month	For the remainder of the month
8. At this point in time	*Now* or *currently*
9. I trust	No trust is involved—use *I suppose* or *I am sure*.
10. At your earliest convenience	Name a specific date.
11. Thank you in advance	It may be presumptuous to assume a response.
12. Take necessary action	*Act*
13. Make a concerted effort to	*Try to*
14. Do not hesitate to call	*Call me if you need*
15. Enclosed please find	*Enclosed is*
16. Attached hereto (herewith)	*Attached*

<table>
<tr><td colspan="2" style="text-align:center">**ACTIVITY 9.1**</td></tr>
</table>

Directions: In each of the following sentences, circle the outdated expressions and write in corrections.

1. Pursuant to your request, I am forwarding your invoice directly to our accounting department for payment.

2. At this point in time, our schedule is progressing as planned.

3. Please be advised that in accordance with the city building regulations, a soil engineer will have to inspect your property.

4. Attached hereto is a copy of the regulations that apply to your building project. I suggest you make a concerted effort to follow these closely to avoid possible legal problems.

REDUNDANCIES

The term **redundant** means "needlessly repetitive"—clearly at odds with the important goal of writing concisely. Many redundant expressions are commonly used. Improve your writing by learning to spot and eliminate redundancies.

<table>
<tr><td colspan="2" style="text-align:center">**ACTIVITY 9.2**</td></tr>
</table>

Part A

Directions: Review the following redundancies, and circle the numbers of any that you have used. Start now to improve your writing by eliminating these redundant terms.

Instead of:	Try:
1. absolutely complete	complete
2. advance planning	planning
3. true facts	facts
4. assembled together	assembled
5. another alternative	an alternative

ACTIVITY 9.2 (continued)

Instead of:	Try:
6. basic fundamentals	fundamentals
7. continue on	continue
8. cooperate together	cooperate
9. each and every	(use one or the other)
10. end result	result
11. open up	open
12. refer back	refer
13. repeat again	repeat
14. at that point in time	at that time
15. my personal opinion	my opinion
16. equally as good as	as good as
17. depreciated in value	depreciate
18. return back to	return to
19. join together	join
20. the two twins	the twins

Part B

Directions: In the following sentences, draw a line through the redundant expressions and insert appropriate revisions.

1. He will arrive at approximately 9:30 a.m. in the morning.

2. Refer back to the purchasing specifications to prepare your requisitions accurately.

3. Everyone voted for the bill, which was passed unanimously.

4. Please take immediate action at once.

5. We have the best previously owned used vehicles, cars, and trucks in all of the entire Tristate Area.

LONG-WINDED AND ABSTRACT TERMS

Pompous, overly abstract, and long-winded terms don't enhance business communications or impress readers. Such terms diminish the clarity and force of your writing. They can also frustrate or confuse readers, particularly in the increasingly international workplace.

Mark Twain captured this idea well: "I never use a word like *metropolis* when I can get the same price for *city*."

In some cases, the best word may be a longer one that conveys the precise meaning required for the situation. However, the words you use should be clear to the reader. Typically, simple words are most effective for business communications. The word *bombastic* is a prime example of a long-winded word; the better choice would be *overblown*. One of the most powerful speeches ever written contains only 257 words, and 196 of those words have only one syllable—Abraham Lincoln's *Gettysburg Address*.

ACTIVITY 9.3

Directions: For each of the following words, write a better choice.

Overworded	Better
initiate	_____
disseminate	_____
finalize	_____
ascertain	_____
utilize	_____
transmit	_____
procure	_____
endeavor	_____
equitable	_____

SPECIFIC, MEASURABLE TERMS

Search for words that help your reader understand, even feel, precisely what you intend. Increase clarity by using measurable terms where appropriate, including numbers and percentages. Choose words that are exact and that project energy; avoid general, vague, and dull words. Note how the specific terms below and on the next page create more vivid and effective images that enhance clarity.

General/Vague/Boring	Specific/Clear
a **good** technician	a **highly skilled** technician
several of our team members	**90 percent** of our team members
a **large** sale	a **$400,000** sale
an **important** issue	a **life-threatening** issue

the **thing** I want to discuss   the **marketing plan** I want to discuss
a **fast** printer   a **24-page-per-minute laser** printer
a **high-resolution** scanner   a **4800-bit** scanner

QUALIFIERS

Eliminate qualifiers—words that unnecessarily minimize your meaning and diminish the credibility of your words. Note how the qualifiers (boldfaced type) in the left column weaken or minimize the message.

Qualified/Weak	Not Qualified/Strong
My work is **quite** good.	My work is good.
I'm **just** a student.	I'm a student.
You'll **probably** like this.	You'll like this.
I'm **sort of (kind of)** enthused.	I'm enthused.
I prepared a **little** summary for you.	I prepared a summary for you.
I'll try to be there.	I will be there.

PROOF POINT!

Directions: In the following sentences, mark corrections in use of redundancies, outdated expressions, qualifiers, and overly general terms.

1. Thank you for your donation. Enclosed please find two tickets for the State Charity Banquet.

2. This is a pretty nice house, and it has been on the market for only one week.

3. I need heavy construction paper.

4. The architectural committee will review your proposed plan during the next scheduled meeting.

5. We think this new product will help us get a foot in the door in our new sales territory.

CHAPTER 10

Professional Finishing Tools

Objective

After completing Chapter 10, you will be able to:

- Proofread and edit to polish final content.

PROOFREADING AND EDITING OF FINAL CONTENT

Proofreading and editing is the process of reviewing your writing, polishing the rough edges, and paying attention to details. These details may be subtle, but they can determine the success or failure of your message. This process of reviewing, critiquing, and revising a message is the step required to produce professional written documents.

Proofread and Edit in Three Steps

Use a three-step method to proofread and edit documents efficiently and accurately. Proofread each document three times, focusing first on format, then on content, and finally on mechanics (grammar, punctuation, and spelling). By concentrating on one aspect at a time, you avoid the possibility of overlooking other elements. For example, when you try to proofread one time for every type of error, you can easily overlook a punctuation or formatting error while concentrating on the content (and vice versa). Concentrating on one aspect at a time increases accuracy and actually decreases production time by eliminating oversights that need correction later.

Follow these three steps when proofreading:

1. **Proofread and edit for accuracy of format.** Check for the following items:

   - Inclusion of required parts, such as the date, inside address, salutation, subject line, body, complimentary close, name/title of writer, enclosure and copy notations, and labeling of subsequent pages

   - Consistent layout (fonts, white space, margins, headings, hanging indentation, lists, page numbering, headers and footers, and graphics)

2. **Proofread and edit the content.** (See the next section, "Edit for Content," for specific editing procedures.) Check for the following items:

- Errors in logic (general message, facts, and contradictions)

- Poor wording (wordiness or overgeneralizations, redundancies, qualifiers, and outdated terms)

3. **Proofread and edit for accuracy of mechanics.** Check for the following items:

- Parallel structure, "stacks of nouns," and subject and verb agreement errors

- Active and passive voice, dummy subjects, camouflaged verbs, and unclear pronoun references

- Grammar usage, sentence and paragraph structure, transitions, punctuation, and spelling

Edit for Content

Print a hard copy of your document, and mark your proofreading and editorial changes on this copy. You can overlook many errors when trying to proofread and edit from the computer screen. Review and critique the entire draft carefully, using a red pen to mark revisions. If possible, read the document to a colleague to help spot errors in content flow. Then edit the message once more considering the following:

1. **The Message.** Is my main message clear? (Apply the "What I'm trying to say here" test to your document. Is it perfectly clear?)

2. **Tone and Voice.** Is the tone and voice too stuffy or too informal? Is the style positive, or does it project a negative tone (rude, curt, wimpy, or condescending)? Have I used the active voice to emphasize? Have I used it as the predominant style? Have I used the passive voice to de-emphasize when necessary?

3. **Reader Viewpoint.** Have I addressed the reader's point of view or just mine? Have I emphasized benefits to the reader?

4. **Conciseness.** Is the message concise? Have I used the fewest possible words to convey my message? Have I used short sentences and paragraphs? Have I eliminated all irrelevant information?

5. **Clarity.** Do any of the sections need to be reworded to avoid confusion?

6. **Logic.** Do my ideas flow smoothly from sentence to sentence and from paragraph to paragraph? Can I add transitional phrases to help the reader tie the ideas together?

7. **Completeness.** Have I omitted information the reader needs to take the appropriate action or make the appropriate response? Have I answered the questions *Who? What? Why? Where? When? How?* and *How much?*

8. **Credibility.** Are my arguments supported with enough convincing facts and details? Have I included graphs, tables, or illustrations and other pertinent material?

9. **Opening and Closing.** Do the opening and closing emphasize the key points? Is the opening positive? Is it worded well?

10. **Call for Action.** Will my reader know what action he or she should take and what deadlines apply (if any)?

Revise Weak Areas

After proofreading and marking corrections on your document, revise and rewrite the content that needs refining to convey the message you want.

1. Break up paragraphs and sentences that are too long.

2. Reword sections that ramble or that don't make sense.

3. Revise to improve emphasis as necessary.

4. Strengthen your arguments if necessary.

5. Improve clarity by using more specific, measurable terms where appropriate, including numbers and percentages.

Edit for Logic and Completeness

Review your document to identify any problems with logic or completeness. Correct errors in logical flow of the message by revising the sequence and adding or deleting content as necessary. Read carefully, considering how much information is necessary to communicate clearly with your reader. Look for these errors:

- Incomplete or missing information

- Incorrect facts or contradictions

- Inconsistencies or sequencing errors

Edit for Correctness

Aim to convey a professional image in your written communications. Once you've polished your message for clarity, conciseness, tone, logic, and emphasis, look for correctness. Check carefully for the following:

- **Errors in wording.** Look for redundancies, outdated phrases, overly general wording, and negative terms.

- **Errors in grammar and structure.** Look for errors in placement of modifiers, use of active and passive voice, use of parallel structure, pronoun/antecedent agreement, and "stacks of nouns."

- **Errors in spelling and punctuation and improved word choice.** Run the spelling and grammar checker; and use the online thesaurus to improve word choice, if necessary. Remember, however, that *you* need to do the final proofreading—no automated system catches all errors. Use a dictionary and a good grammar reference as resources.

Follow Formatting and Printing Guidelines

The way your document looks can enhance or diminish the effectiveness of your writing. At first glance, based on the general appearance of your letter, the reader will make a conscious or subconscious judgment about you and your organization. You can be sure this first impression is positive by applying these techniques:

- **Use a standard business format.** Refer to the document formats in Chapter 9. Business professionals expect to receive written communications that are formatted correctly. Make sure your documents follow correct formatting guidelines.

- **Use a readable font.** Don't use a font smaller than 12 point. Times New Roman is a good choice for the body of documents because the serif style is easy to read. To provide a contrast, you may want to use a different font for headings, such as Arial. However, using several different fonts in one document creates an unprofessional, cluttered look.

- **Use white space.** White space refers to the areas in a document that have no text or graphics—just blank, open white space. Don't crowd your document with too much printed matter. Allow for adequate margins (top, bottom, and sides) and space between document parts, which add visual appeal.

- **Use printing enhancements.** To emphasize ideas or items, use headings, bold-faced type, underlining, all capital letters, bullets, alternate print styles, and graphics (pictures, lines, boxes, bar graphs, and charts). Don't overuse these enhancements, or your document will look too busy.

Seek Another Perspective

To polish a critical message, ask a colleague to read it aloud to you. Getting another perspective and listening to the message are effective ways to pinpoint elusive or subtle problems and to turn out a top-notch piece of writing.

PROOF POINT!

Directions: Proofread and edit your copy of your Power Tools Writing Project (assigned during the first session of this course). Proofread your assignment carefully, and mark corrections to the types of errors you have learned to avoid. Those covered in this course are listed below.

1. Write complete sentences, and correct errors in subject and verb agreement.

2. Correct inappropriate use of active and passive voice.

PROOF POINT! (continued)

3. Eliminate dummy subjects (*there* or *it* followed by *to be* used as the subject).

   No: **There are** three candidates qualified for the position.

   Yes: Three candidates are qualified for the position.

4. Eliminate camouflaged verbs, such as "I will **make a decision.**"

5. Correct errors in the use of commas, colons, and semicolons.

6. Correct parallel structure errors (use *ing* with *ing,* verbs with verbs, and *to* with *to*).

7. Correct misplaced modifiers; for example, "They stopped when the car over-heated and asked for water."

   - Eliminate pronoun errors (antecedent agreement and clarity of reference). "The supervisor told the employee **he** should call at 4 p.m." (Who should call?)
   - "Remove the printers from the cartons, and leave **them** on the loading dock." (Leave what—the printers or the cartons?)

8. Eliminate "stacks of nouns" (more than three in a row).

9. Improve the tone, if necessary. Eliminate negative or discourteous words. Include terms that are personal or that convey empathy, as appropriate.

10. Address the needs of the reader (not just your own or those of your organization).

11. Break up paragraphs and sentences that are too long.

12. Add word and graphic transitions, as needed, to enhance readability.

    - Words that link ideas (*therefore, following, in addition*)
    - Headings, lists, and graphics

13. If the message is best organized in the direct pattern:

    - Use a clear subject line.
    - Clarify the purpose and discuss benefits in the first paragraph.
    - Discuss benefits up front.

14. When using the indirect pattern, do not lead with the main purpose of your message.

15. When writing to persuade, state the main argument and support it with evidence.

16. Use an appropriate document format for your message (e-mail, memo, or letter).

17. Eliminate outdated terms (*as per*), redundancies (*open up*), and qualifiers (*a little*).

18. Edit to correct errors in logical flow of the message by revising sequence and adding or deleting content as necessary.

19. Edit to provide specific details necessary for clarity and effectiveness. Use specific words and measurable terms, including numbers and percentages. Edit to correct errors in spelling.

20. Ask a colleague to read an important document aloud to you.

APPENDIX

- Assess Your Writing
- Internet Resources
- Proofreaders' Marks
- Power Tools Writing Project
- Practice Posttest
- Quick References 1, 2, 3, and 4

ASSESS YOUR WRITING: DOES IT MEET BUSINESS STANDARDS?

Directions: On a scale of one to ten, rate your ability in each of the following business writing areas. A rating of one is lowest, and a rating of ten is highest.

On the first class day: Rate yourself in the Precourse Rating column.

On the last class day: Rate yourself in the Postcourse Rating column.

Business Writing Standard	Precourse Rating	Postcourse Rating
1. Correct document formatting	_____	_____
2. Correct use of grammar and punctuation	_____	_____
3. Correct sentence and paragraph structure	_____	_____
4. Appropriate organization of message content	_____	_____
5. Complete content	_____	_____
6. Skillful use of tone	_____	_____
7. Skillful use of voice	_____	_____
8. Use of clear, specific terms	_____	_____
9. Elimination of redundancies and clichés	_____	_____
10. Proofreading and editing to polish final documents	_____	_____

INTERNET WRITING RESOURCES

The following web sites are useful for learning more about writing development. Many of these sites offer additional exercises to help you strengthen several of the skills presented in *Power Tools for Business Writing*. Some of these sites offer information and exercises on expanded writing topics as well as more elementary content dealing with grammar development.

http://andromeda.rutgers.edu/%7Ejlynch/Writing/index.html

http://www.ccc.commnet.edu/grammar

http://dictionary.reference.com

http://www.editavenue.com/writing_tips_articles_1.asp

http://occawlonline.pearsoned.com/bookbind/pubbooks/long_longman_uoplezap_1/index.html

http://owl.english.purdue.edu

http://owl.english.purdue.edu/internet/owls/writing-labs.html

http://powa.org

http://rwc.hunter.cuny.edu/writing/on-line.html

http://www.webwritingthatworks.com

PROOFREADERS' MARKS

Mark		Example	Mark		Example
#	Add space	in theoffice	=	Insert hyphen	Thirty three
‖	Align vertically	Mr. Martin Lopez P.O. Box 3216 Wichita, KS 67207-1171	⊙	Insert period	Ms Cormier
			/	Lowercase	Monthly Figures
			∿	Make bold	Heading
≡	Capitalize	in phoenix	∫	Move as shown	Send the proposal by Tuesday to Chris.
		Sales Report			
] [	Center	ANNUAL REPORT	[	Move left	He sent the invoice.
—	Change word	fee cost estimate	]	Move right	$44,688.46
⌒	Close up space	inter esting	ss[	Single-space	She is writing the training book.
⌿	Delete	content			
		as well as well as	sp ◯	Spell out	sp 2 days sp Nov 20
ᴅs[	Double-space	We will meet in his office.			
			¶	Start new paragraph	We increased fees. ¶ Hire two new aids.
∧	Insert	Reshedule the call office	stet	Stet (Leave as originally written)	Wednesday on Tuesday stet
∧	Insert comma	Atlanta Georgia	∿	Transpose	adn

POWER TOOLS WRITING PROJECT

Follow the directions below to complete the Power Tools Writing Project, the main assignment for this course. This assignment is designed to improve your writing through proofreading and editing exercises you will apply to this document on the last day of class.

1. Write a one- to two-page document. Format the document using double space.

2. Choose a significant topic. (See the topic choices listed below.)

3. Cluster your topic to generate key ideas to be developed in your assignment.

4. Review your cluster, and add or delete items as necessary.

5. Number your ideas in order of appropriate sequence for development of the message.

6. Write a focus statement that summarizes your entire message in as few words as possible.

7. Develop a rough draft of your document based on your clustered items.

8. Revise and polish your draft to prepare your completed writing assignment.

9. On the second day of class, give one copy of your completed assignment to your instructor. Retain the other copy to use on the last day of class. Your instructor will explain this exercise.

TOPIC CHOICES

- Select a topic of your choice—a real document you want or need to write. (This is the most useful topic, as you will benefit most by analyzing the type of writing you are typically required to produce.)

- Write a proposal or recommendation you want to make regarding your work or some other meaningful activity in which you are involved.

- Write a request for something from your superior, such as equipment, training, or new assignments.

- Write a letter to the editor of your newsletter regarding a topic you are interested in developing.

PRACTICE POSTTEST

Commas, Colons, Semicolons, Clear Pronoun References
Directions: Insert commas, colons, and semicolons; and correct any unclear pronoun references.

1. We plan to consider the following four budget items during our next meeting training needs conference topics software upgrades and advertising. Please prepare a cover letter and a list of the priorities for your department. Give a copy of it to your team members for review. When we meet next week I will give each of you ten minutes to summarize the priorities of your team however I expect you to be fully prepared to discuss all of the items in detail.

Direct Pattern Content
Directions: What two items should be included in the first paragraph of a message written in the direct pattern?

2. _____   _____

Dummy Subjects and Camouflaged Verbs
Directions: Revise to eliminate dummy subjects and camouflaged verbs. Each sentence contains both types of errors.

3. There are six topics he plans to vote on, and I will make the suggestion that we table two of these.

4. It is her duty to conduct inspections of all processing plants in this region.

Active and Passive Voice
Directions: Revise using active and passive voice effectively.

5. A 25 percent increase in sales was achieved by our office this year.

6. We made a calibration error in our laboratory.

Parallel Structure
Directions: Revise to make the elements parallel in structure.

7. He expects to travel to Mexico, to meet with the Guadalajara site executives, and he will review our business plan with them.

8. The editorial team reviewed the production process, researched strategies for improvement, and by the original deadline.

Misplaced Modifiers
Directions: Revise to correct the misplaced modifier.

9. Our manager outlined his entire presentation while traveling from Florida to California in one hour.

Subject and Verb Agreement
Directions: Circle the correct verb.

10. The envelope containing two copies of all receipts for these projects (is, are) ready for mailing.

11. Each of the quarterly reports and proposals (was, were) copied and mailed to you today

Tone
Directions: Revise to create a more positive or personal tone.

12. We cannot ship your order until September 15.

E-mail
Directions: Circle the correct answer.

13. The appropriate font size for e-mail messages is 10-point.

    a. true   b. false

Document Formats
Directions: Circle the correct answer.

14. Using lists and headings is appropriate for emphasizing content in letters, memos, and e-mail messages.

    a. true   b. false

Word Choice
Directions: Revise to eliminate redundancies, outdated terms, and unnecessary qualifiers.

15. Enclosed please find the sales data we assembled together for your review. This report is quite complete and addresses the requirements you specified.

Proofreading
Directions: Circle the correct answer.

16. Proofreading entirely from the computer screen is the most efficient way to find errors.

    a. true   b. false